Modern Russian Songs

Ernest Newman

MODERN
RUSSIAN SONGS

EDITED BY ERNEST NEWMAN

VOLUME I

ALPHERAKY TO MOUSSORGSKY

FOR HIGH VOICE

BOSTON: OLIVER DITSON COMPANY

NEW YORK: CHAS. H. DITSON & CO. CHICAGO: LYON & HEALY

CONTENTS

CONTENTS

INDEX

INDEX

BALAKIREFF

BLEICHMANN

ARENSKY

CUI

EIGHT
RUSSIAN
COMPOSERS

IPPOLITOFF-IVANOFF

GLINKA

GRETCHANINOFF

BORODINE

THE RUSSIAN SONG

THE thesaurus of Russian song is the second richest in Europe in one respect, and the first in another. Every country has, of course, an abundance of musical lyrics. But it will hardly be disputed by any one that the Germanic races have produced the largest number of art songs of the highest class; and it will probably be admitted by every one who has given any study to the subject that the Russian treasury of song surpasses even the German in variety, if not in quantity. Vast as the German output has been, and varied as have been the minds that have expressed themselves in the song, the family likenesses overbear, on the whole, the personal differences: there is an unmistakable something that is common to Schubert, Schumann, Brahms, Wolf, Jensen, Franz, Strauss, Mahler, and a hundred others. These family likenesses, it is true, will be found in the songs of every race, and it goes without saying that they exist in the Russian song. None the less true is it, I think, that the personal characteristics are more marked there than in the German song: to pass from Glinka to Borodine, from Borodine to Moussorgsky, from Moussorgsky to Rachmaninoff, from Rachmaninoff to Stravinsky, from Stravinsky to Arensky, from Arensky to Liapounoff, from Liapounoff to Medtner, from Medtner to Vassilenko, from Vassilenko to Tchaïkovsky, from Tchaïkovsky to Tcherepnin, and so on through a score of other names, is to see a more sharply differentiated set of physiognomies than when we pass from Schubert to Schumann, from Schumann to Mahler, from Mahler to Strauss, from Strauss to Wolf, from Wolf to Loewe. And the remarkable thing is that this unusually rich crop of song has been sown and reaped in much less than a century. There were Russian and pseudo-Russian song composers before Glinka: one pre-Glinka song, the "Nightingale" of Alabieff (1802–1852), is still occasionally sung. But to all intents and purposes the Russian song begins with Glinka (1804–1857). The earliest of his songs date from his teens, but the bulk of them—and certainly the best of them—were written after he was thirty: of the two included in the present collection, "The Star of the North" belongs to 1839, "The Journey" to 1840. ("A Life for the Czar," it will be remembered, was produced in 1836, and "Rousslan and Ludmilla" in 1842.) Schubert's "Erl King" was written in 1815, and there had been a long and honorable line of German song composers before Schubert; a masterpiece like the "Erl King," indeed, could come only as the crown of a long tradition, whereas even the best songs of Glinka are no more than a beginning.

II

THE variety of style of the Russian song is the result of the variety of influences, racial, local, and cultural, to which it has been subject. German art song has drunk as deeply of the fountain of folksong; but German art music and German folk music have always been so intimately associated that it is hard to say where the one ends and the other begins. It is not so much that the folk music has been an influence upon the composers as that it has been part of their bone and blood and being. The moods, the prosody, the structure, the cadence of the folksong run, broadly speaking, through almost all the German music, sacred and secular, vocal and instrumental, of the last three hundred years The music and the poetry of the race developed hand in hand. We have only to turn over a German anthology of poetry to see that the poetic rhythms of five hundred years ago, whether they be those of folk poets or of art poets, are the same as those of Heine and Goethe and Heyse and Eichendorff and Dehmel; and until Hugo Wolf enlarged the rhythmic boundaries of the German song, it followed, in general, the metrical models of the folksong of centuries ago.

In Russia the evolution was different. Russian folk music had existed long before Russian art music came into being; with the result that when the composers fell under its spell, it became a genuine *influence* of which they were more or less conscious. Art music as the German musician of the mid-nineteenth century knew it could not go to the German folksong for inspiration, for it had never really quitted it. But the Russian composer who, having learned his technique and imbibed a good part of his idiom from the Western music of his day, turned then to his native folk music, found in it an inexhaustible treasure-house of novelty. Thus we can speak of a genuine *influence* of Russian folksong upon Russian art song.

III

RUSSIAN music, again, was fortunate in that it had no national cultural tradition of its own so overwhelming that there was no escape from it—no thought of escape from it. German music, on the whole, has been self-contained for many generations: each young composer has drunk in the one great German tradition as naturally and unconsciously as he breathed in the German air. The tradition, the culture, were uniform for the whole political area. The Russian escaped this uniformity of influence. On the one hand, as we have seen, there were the treasures of folksong to draw upon. On the other, there was, in addition to marked local differences of race and tradition, a strong Oriental or quasi-Oriental influence. A Croatian composer like Haydn, a Bohemian composer like Gluck, are drawn so deeply into the German tradition that they are, in essence, German composers pure and simple. But the Orientalism that has always been part of Russian music has never lost its own characteristics of mood and style; neither it nor the Russian folk style has ever been strong enough to absorb the other. The Russian song composer thus already has two sources of culture to draw upon, as against the German's one; and in addition he has—the German culture. Like his country, he is both in Europe and apart from it. He has his own inner sources of spiritual strength, and he is free to assimilate what he will of the spiritual strength of the rest of Europe. And in music this has meant, in the main, taking the best that the great Germans could give him.

IV

THUS we get three different styles in the Russian song,—the folk style, the Oriental style, and the style that is a distillation from the German song. Sometimes the three are exploited separately; more often they are subtly interblended. (Other styles also are found, but they are personal rather than communal—the quasi-recitative of Dargomijsky, for instance, the Moussorgsky songs that get as close as possible to the rhythms and accents of speech, and the post-impressionist style, as we may perhaps call it, of the later Stravinsky. These are not represented in the present volumes.)

From the beginning the Russian song showed a good deal of variety. Glinka has one ear always open to folksong; but he never quite forgets the suave Italian style in which he was brought up. His successor Dargomijsky fluctuates between Italianism, Orientalism, Muscovitism, eclecticism, and something that is absolutely his own. The "Five" (Cui, Borodine, Rimsky-Korsakoff, Moussorgsky, and Balakireff) exhibit far more variety than the contemporary German song can show. When the nationalist impulse of the '50s and '60s weakened, Russian song composers went each his own way, some of them still writing deliberately in the folk style, others feeling the folk style more or less unconsciously as a stimulus, still others, like Medtner, ignoring it completely. Only the theorist will cry out against composers of this last type. The plain man will decide that it does not matter in the least in what style a musician writes, so long as it is a good style. An artist can express finely only what he has felt deeply; and if a composer finds himself more responsive to the culture of another nation than to the popular life of his own, we have no right to say him nay. If it is objected that Medtner's songs are not Russian but German, the sufficient answer is that, whatever section of the map they may set us thinking about, they are first-rate. No doubt a German might have written them, but as a matter of fact no German did; and it is better for us that they should have been written by a Russian than not written at all. A man must be allowed to choose his own loves and friendships in art as in private life. If Medtner prefers to spend his time talking to Goethe and Heine and Brahms and Wolf, rather than in freezing his toes watching the Russian peasant doing his frog dance in the snow, that is purely his affair. To do anything else would be insincerity on his part; and out of insincerity no great art can come.

V

MEDTNER shows practically no trace of "nationalism." Most of the others exhibit it in one form or another, one degree or another. Sometimes a song is deliberately couched in the folk idiom: perhaps the most thoroughgoing example of this in the present collection is the "Parrot Song" of Moussorgsky (from *Boris Godounoff*)—which is none the less a song for being contained in an opera. Sometimes we are conscious of the Russian people in the song, even though the phrases may not, in the main, specifically copy the folk style; the suggestion is psychological rather than tonal. To this class belong Moussorgsky's "Savishna" and "Gathering Mushrooms;" they bring up Russia before our eyes, not so much by the use of external apparatus, such as scales or cadences, but by painting the folk from the life. In this sphere, indeed, Moussorgsky still stands alone. No composer in any country has been so thoroughly of the people in his sympathies and in his art. For Moussorgsky, folksong was not, as it is for most composers, an exotic, a *sauce piquante,* with which to dash the common musical idiom now and then, but the expression of the very soul of the people—not the people as the town-dweller sees them, half sympathetically, half condescendingly, but as they see themselves. Moussorgsky felt their few joys and their many sorrows as no other composer has done; and the intensity of his absorption in them made him speak their own musical tongue, but speak it as a genius of the people would do.

He had the painter's eye and the novelist's breadth of sympathy. He joined hands on one side with Verestchagin, on the other with Dostoievsky. His was the period of intense national consciousness and aspiration, of sympathy on the part of the intelligentsia with the poor and oppressed. The "Savishna" is a human document without an analogue in any other song literature. One day, from the window of the country house in which he was staying, he looked out of the window and saw the village idiot begging the love of the village beauty, and being repulsed with scorn for his hideousness and poverty. The wave of pity that surged through Moussorgsky found voice in "Savishna;" the words as well as the music are his. The song is, on the whole, the finest example of his realism. He has hit upon a $\frac{5}{4}$ rhythm that well expresses the urgency of the peasant's appeal: the absence of a single quaver's rest anywhere in the song suggests the panting breathlessness of his long cry; and it finishes without a formal ending,—the breath just goes out of him, and that is the end, with the song still suspended, question-like, in the air.

VI

Moussorgsky gives us better than any one else both the direct imitation of folksong and the sublimation of this into art song. Of the latter, the finest specimens, apart from "Savishna," are "Gathering Mushrooms" and the "Hopak." Here the slight touch of peasant harshness that we are conscious of in such songs as the "Trepak" disappears. These songs, too, are better built than some of the realistic ones: they have a perfection of form—particularly "Gathering Mushrooms"—that reminds us of the greatest German songs.

The folksong influence, as I have said, shows itself in various ways in the other composers. The folk style will always be found, employed deliberately, when the Russian people are the subject of the poem. We see it, for instance, in Cui's "Hunger Song," Kopyloff's "The Laborer's Plaint," and Wihtol's "Beggar's Song." Russian popular song has often a curious monotony of phrase, as if the idea in the singer's mind were an obsession, as if the complete giving up of the soul to the one feeling had almost numbed the faculty of speech. It is with this monotony, this hammering on the one idea, that Moussorgsky and the other writers of the song of social sympathy, as we may call it, make their most poignant effects.

In other cases the folk idiom enters quite unconsciously into the style of the composer, as a local peculiarity of accent will sometimes show in the speech of a man who otherwise speaks the standardized tongue of the capital. It is the purely Russian touch that we get, for example, in measures 7 and 8 of Bagrinofski's "All the Bells;" and the reader will detect a hundred other touches of the same kind in other songs. Often the Russian flavor comes from peculiar rhythms that are not found in the songs of any other race; these rhythms in their turn are conditioned by the prosody and inflections of the language.

The influence of the build of a language upon the rhythms of the music of a country has never been sufficiently investigated. It is tolerably clear that one of the most familiar phrase-endings of Spanish music—this, from Granados's "Goyescas"—

has come into being through the richness of the Spanish language in double rhymes,—*muerto, cierto, amante, anhelante, amores, flores, mundo, profundo,* and so on. The process may be seen at work in the following passages from Granados's songs "La Maja dolorosa:"

Double rhymes being scarce in English (except in present participles), it is not surprising that this peculiar effect, as of the shooting of the same bolt upon a pair of phrases, is not one of the characteristics of English melody.

Russian prosody has had a good deal of influence on Russian melody. Russian poetry is rich in dactylic endings—which, needless to say, set the English translator insoluble problems at times. These dactyls often end in a vowel—another thorn in the side of the translator, for the vowel-ending gives a peculiar lightness to the finish of the Russian phrase that cannot be duplicated in English. I once had this forcibly brought home to me by hearing a Czech choir sing "God save the Queen" (in their own tongue). Each two-measure phrase tapered off like the thin end of a wedge; with us, from the very nature of the words, the emphasis on each note is the same. The difference between the all-through blunt effect and the tapering effect in the dactyl may be illustrated by the unvarying lumpishness of the consonantal "gracious Queen" or "walking-stick"—which some people would not even class as dactyls, but as feet of three longs—and the airiness, the dive and float, of "Arcady" or "mystery."

With these illustrations in mind, let the reader now look at Liapounoff's "Christmas Song." The Russian text of the first eight measures, corresponding to the English words—

"Little song of Christmastide,
Tuneful in its dulcet sound
Like unto a string of pearls
Radiant on a velvet ground,"

may be roughly transliterated thus—

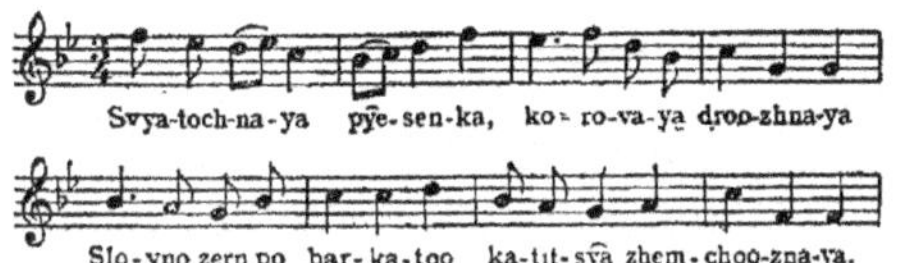

It will be seen that the most expert choice of English words cannot quite reproduce the lilt of the original, the soft vowel-endings of the lines, the tapering of the verbal sound that suggests to the singer a corresponding tapering of the melodic phrase. The geniuses of the two languages are absolutely different. I draw attention to the fact here not only to show how gallantly the translators have braved these and other difficulties, but to indicate, *en passant*, the correct phrasing (because the natural phrasing) of the melodies, and to show how, in many cases, a type of melody that strikes the ear at once as being peculiarly Russian has come about not through any conscious desire of the composer to imitate a folk idiom, but purely and simply as the result of the "pull" of the words.

The same phenomenon is met with again in Kalinnikoff's "Stars Ethereal," where the opening Russian words run thus (two measures to a line).

Zvezdi yasneya, zvezdi prikrasniya
Nashentali tsvetam skazki choodniya.

Vocal rhythms such as those of Tcherepnin's "Stars of Radiant Night" and Moussorgsky's "Ah, not with God's Thunder," again, will not be found in the songs of any other race: they are motived and conditioned by the genius of the Russian language.

VII

With these general remarks on the style and the scope of the Russian song, the reader may now be left to find his own enjoyment in working through the present volumes. There is something for all tastes. Even on what may be called, without offence, the lower slopes, the vintage is better than in most countries. There is always room for the song that, without any pretence of profundity of philosophy or science of technique, gives voice to the simple, honest feelings of simple, honest people. There is no need for this sort of thing to degenerate into the bleating sentimentality of the worst German, the anaemic thinness of the worst French, or the devastating vulgarity of the worst English song. Men like Alpheraky can be popular without being inane. The cosmopolitan Russian composers, such as Arensky, Taneieff, Rubinstein, Tchaïkovsky, and Gretchaninoff, still have a Russian touch somewhere or other about them. Medtner falls into line with the greatest of the German song writers: Hugo Wolf himself would not have disdained to sign a song like "Solitude." Liapounoff, like Medtner, is an accomplished writer for the piano, and his accompaniments profit by his double gift. Rimsky-Korsakoff exhibits in his songs the same range of interests, the same variety of styles, and the same sensitiveness to beauty, as in his operas and instrumental works. Rachmaninoff, like Medtner and Liapounoff, fertilizes his lyric style by his genius for the piano, and limns his peculiarly serious physiognomy as unerringly in his smaller as in his larger works. Tcherepnin, Vassilenko, and Sachnofsky illustrate some of the newer phases of the Russian song, with its surety of technique placed at the service of a generous eclecticism of interest. Stravinsky is represented by a song of his youth, in which the discriminating ear can catch many a prophecy of the later Stravinsky. All in all, the songs here presented give, it is hoped, an adequate idea of the extraordinary richness of a development that has been crowded into but little over three quarters of a century,—the most marvellous record that the song can show in any European country in the same space of time.

Ernest Newman.

BIOGRAPHICAL SKETCHES

ALPHERAKY, ACHILLES NIKOLAIEVITCH

Born at Charkov, June 21, 1846. Was at one time attached to the Czar's court. He has written an opera, piano pieces, songs, etc.

ARENSKY, ANTON STEPANOVITCH

Born at Novgorod, July 31, 1861. Both his parents were musical. After some preliminary studies under Zikke, he entered Rimsky-Korsakoff's class at the Petrograd Conservatoire (1879–82), in the latter year he was appointed professor of harmony and counterpoint at the Moscow Conservatoire. He became conductor of the Russian Choral Society's concerts in Moscow, and, in 1895, of the Imperial Chapel Choir in Petrograd. He died on February 12, 1906. His works include the successful opera, *A Dream on the Volga* (1890), two other operas, *Raphael* (in one act, 1894) and *Nal and Damayanti* (1899), various cantatas and choruses, much church music, two symphonies, a piano concerto, a piano trio, two string quartets, a piano quintet, a ballet (*Egyptian Night*), a large number of piano pieces and songs, and two books, on harmony and form, respectively.

BAGRINOFSKI, M.

BALAKIREFF, MILI ALEXEIVITCH

Born at Nijni-Novgorod, January 2, 1837. He received his first lessons in music from his mother. In his youth he lived for a time in the country house of Oulibicheff, the biographer of Mozart and author of a book on Beethoven. Oulibicheff had an extensive musical library and maintained a private band, by both of which the student and budding composer profited; he was deeply impressed also by the peasant music of the province. He went to live in Petrograd in 1855, met Glinka, and was soon regarded by the latter—then approaching the end of his days—as his destined successor in the renaissance of Russian music. Gradually Balakireff gathered about himself a number of young enthusiasts inspired by the same nationalistic ideals: a group of five (Balakireff himself, Cui, Moussorgsky, Rimsky-Korsakoff, and Borodine) became known as "The Invincible Band," and worked in harmony for some years, until the varying temperaments of its members led to a certain divergence from each other. Balakireff was an erudite musician and a skilled technician; his influence upon the rest of the group was great.

In 1862 he helped to found the Free School of Music in Petrograd; its concerts were intended to be a progressive counterblast to the more conservative work of the Imperial Musical Society. In 1869 he became conductor of the latter Society and Director of the Imperial Chapel Choir. He retired from the directorship of the Free School of Music in 1873, being succeeded by Rimsky-Korsakoff, from that date until his death at Petrograd, on May 29, 1916, he lived in more or less seclusion, his mind having taken on a markedly mystical cast.

He is best known by his symphonic poem *Thamar*, the piano piece *Islamey*, the *Overture on Russian Themes*, and a symphonic poem *Russia* (written in 1862 for the celebration of the thousandth anniversary of the Russian nation). In addition he wrote an overture to *King Lear*, an *Overture on Czech Themes*, two symphonies, a piano concerto (his last work), a number of piano pieces, and some songs. He also edited two collections of Russian folksongs.

BLEICHMANN, JULIUS IVANOVITCH

Born at Petrograd, December 5, 1868. Studied at the Conservatoire there under Solovieff and Rimsky-Korsakoff; afterwards under Reinecke and Jadassohn in Leipzig. He founded (1893–94) the Petrograd Popular Symphony Concerts and was conductor of the Philharmonic Concerts (1894–95). Died in Petrograd December 5, 1909. His works include two operas, piano pieces, chamber music, orchestral works, songs, etc.

BORODINE, ALEXANDER PORPHYRIEVITCH

Born at Petrograd, October 31, 1834,—the illegitimate son of a Prince of Imeritia (Georgia). His scientific bent asserted itself at an early age. It was decided that he should take up medicine as a career, and to that end he entered the Petrograd Academy of Medicine. In 1856 he received an appointment as surgeon in an army hospital, where he first met Moussorgsky, though the friendship did not ripen till the pair met again after some three years' separation. He took his degree in 1858, and spent from 1859 to 1862 travelling in various European countries at the expense of the Russian Government, studying different medical methods. On his return, in 1862, he was appointed assistant lecturer at the Petrograd Academy of Medicine. His friendship with Balakireff, who influenced him strongly, dates from about this time. He married in 1863, became a lecturer in chemistry, and helped to found the School of Medicine for Women, at which institution he lectured from 1872 till his death, at Petrograd, on February 28, 1887.

He had dabbled in music from childhood: he recognized his amateurishness after his meeting with Balakireff, with whom he made serious studies in technique. His output, for a man who could practise music only in the rare intervals of freedom from quite other professional work, was pretty considerable. His works include an opera *Prince Igor* (left unfinished, but completed by Rimsky-Korsakoff and Glazounoff), two symphonies, a Symphonic Sketch *In the Steppes of Central Asia*, two string quartets, two movements of an unfinished symphony, an unfinished opera-ballet *Mlada*, about a dozen songs, a few piano pieces, etc.

CUI, CÉSAR ANTONOVITCH

Born at Vilna, January 18, 1835. His mother was a Lithuanian, his father a French officer wounded in Napoleon's Russian campaign of 1812 and left behind in the retreat. He studied music at an early age, and in 1849 had some lessons from the Polish composer Moniuzsko. In 1850 he entered the Petrograd School of Military Engineering, where he remained for seven years; at the end of his studentship he became a subprofessor in the School. He afterwards had a distinguished career as a lecturer on fortifications and kindred subjects. Among his pupils were General Skobeleff and the late Czar Nicholas II.

He kept up his music during his engineering studies; and the turning-point in his career as a musician came when he made the acquaintance of Balakireff in 1856. It was under the latter's stimulus that he began to compose. He became one of the "Five," and did a great deal of journalistic work for the nationalistic school — incidentally making a number of enemies for it and for himself. He died in 1918.

He wrote some hundred and thirty songs, a quantity of choral and piano music, eight operas — *The Mandarin's Son* (1859), *The Prisoner of the Caucasus* (1859), *William Ratcliff* (1869), *Angelo* (1876), *The Saracen*, (1889), *The Filibusterer* (1894), *A Feast in Plague-Time*, and *Mam'zelle Fifi* (1903), several works for violin, string quartet, etc., and several for orchestra, of which perhaps the best known is the suite *In Modo Populari*. His book on *Music in Russia* did a great deal to interest Western Europe in Russian music.

DARGOMIJSKY, ALEXANDER SERGEIVITCH

Born in the Government of Toula, February 14, 1813, of well-to-do parents. He received an amateurish musical education as a boy, and began composing at fifteen. In 1831 he entered the Government service, but retired four years later, having kept up his musical studies meanwhile. He met Glinka in 1833, who urged him to a more rigorous study of theory and technique. In 1839 he wrote his first opera *Esmeralda*, which was not produced, however, until 1847 (at Moscow). His next big work, *The Triumph of Bacchus*, was first designed as a cantata (1842), then transformed into an opera ballet (1848). *The Roussalka* followed in 1856. He travelled abroad in 1864, and on his return to Russia joined Balakireff and his friends in the movement for the making of a national school of music. His last opera, *The Stone Guest*, in which he carried out to the full his doctrine of a vocal line that should be part melody, part recitative, was left unfinished at his death in January, 1869, and was completed by Cui and Rimsky-Korsakoff, and produced in February, 1872.

His other works include a few pieces for orchestra (*Kazachok*, *Baba-Yaga*, *The Dance of Mummers*, etc.), and for piano, and many songs, vocal duets, trios, quartets, and choruses.

GLIÈRE, REINHOLD MORISSOVITCH

Born at Kief, January 11, 1875. Studied at the Moscow Conservatoire, under Taneieff, Ippolitoff-Ivanoff, and Hrjimaly (violin), from 1894 to 1900. In 1914 he became director of the Kief Conservatoire. His largest works are three symphonies and a symphonic poem *The Sirens*. The others include two string quartets and other chamber music works, pieces for piano and various other instruments, and a large number of songs.

GLINKA, MICHAIL IVANOVITCH

Born at Novospasskoi, in the Government of Smolensk, June 2, 1804, of rich parents. He received a smattering of musical education at home in childhood, and absorbed many impressions from the folk music of the neighborhood. He was at school in Petrograd from 1817 to 1822, during which time he had a few piano lessons from Field. He took up the violin also, and dabbled in composition without having had any proper technical training. After a period of travel, he settled in Petrograd in 1824, in a government office, took up singing, and continued to compose like an amateur. He resigned his office in 1828, and travelled extensively in Europe during the next few years. In 1833, in Berlin, he went through a systematic study of harmony, counterpoint, and composition, under Dehn.

He returned to Russia in 1834, possessed with the idea of writing a Russian national opera. This was realized in *A Life for the Czar*, which was first performed on November 27, 1836, with immediate success. From 1836 to 1839 he acted as choirmaster in the Imperial Chapel. His second opera, *Rousslan and Ludmilla*, was given in November, 1842. Its cold reception depressed him, and he went abroad again in 1844, travelling principally in France and Spain. In Paris, under the influence of Berlioz, he conceived the ambition of becoming an orchestral composer: his chief works in this line were the *Jota Aragonesa*, the *Night in Madrid*, and the *Kamarinskaya*, all written between 1848 and 1852. He returned, after many wanderings and home-comings, to Petrograd, when the Crimean War broke out in 1854. He visited Berlin again in 1856, and died there on February 3, 1857.

Besides the works above mentioned, he wrote a string quartet, a sextet for piano and strings, a trio for piano, clarinet, and bassoon, and other chamber music works, many piano pieces, choruses, songs, and duets, the incidental music to Count Koukolnik's tragedy *Prince Kholmsky*, etc.

GRETCHANINOFF, ALEXANDER TICHONOVITCH

Born at Moscow, October 13, 1864. He entered the Moscow Conservatoire in 1881, studying under Kashkin, Safonoff (piano), Laroche and Hubert (counterpoint), and Arensky (harmony) Later he took lessons from Taneieff, and entered the Petrograd Conservatoire in 1890, where he worked under Rimsky-Korsakoff. He returned to Moscow in 1896. Here his opera *Dobrinya Nikitich* (begun in 1895) was performed in 1903 His other works include an opera on Maeterlinck's *Sister Beatrice*, two symphonies, a piano trio, a setting of Ostrovsky's *Snow-Maiden*, and many songs.

IPPOLITOFF-IVANOFF, MICHAIL MICHAILOVITCH

(Ippolitoff was his mother's name. He added the prefix because there was another Michail Michailovitch Ivanoff.) Born at Gatschina, November 19, 1859. Was at the Petrograd Conservatoire from 1875 to 1882 under Rimsky-Korsakoff (composition). In the latter year he became director of the Music School, and conductor of the Symphony Concerts of the Imperial Russian Musical Society at Tiflis In 1884 he became conductor also of the opera there. Settled in Moscow in 1893 as professor of composition at the Conservatoire. Six years later he became conductor of the Moscow Private Opera. He has composed several operas, —*Ruth* (Tiflis, 1887), *Assya* (Moscow, 1900), *The Betrayal* (Moscow, 1911), etc.,—cantatas and other choral works, overtures (*Yar Khmel*, *Spring*, *Medea*), a symphony, the well-known suite *Caucasian Sketches*, a piano quartet, a string quartet, and several songs. He has written books on harmony and on the folksongs of Georgia.

JACOBSON, MYRON

KALINNIKOFF, BASIL SERGEIVITCH

Born January 13, 1866, at Voina, in the Government of Orlov. Educated at the Orlovsky Seminary. In 1884 he entered the Music School of the Moscow Philharmonic Society, studying the bassoon and composition under Ilyinsky and Blaramberg. He left the school in 1892, and in the season 1893–94 acted as second conductor at the Moscow Italian Opera. His health giving way, he had to go to the South. He died of consumption at Jalta, January 11, 1901. He is best known abroad by his first symphony, in G minor. In addition to this he wrote a second symphony, various other orchestral works, a string quartet, a cantata (*St. John Damascene*), overture and incidental music to Tolstoi's play *Czar Boris*, symphonic poems (*The Nymphs* and *Cedar and Palm*), a ballad for soli, chorus, and orchestra (*The Roussalka*), piano pieces, and songs.

KOPYLOFF, ALEXANDER

Born July 14, 1854. Has written a symphony, an overture, an orchestral scherzo, two string quartets, songs, etc.

KORESTSCHENKO, ARSENI NIKOLAIEVITCH

Born December 18, 1870. Studied at the Moscow Conservatoire under Taneieff and Arensky. From 1891 taught counterpoint and form at the Conservatoire. His works include the operas *Belshazzar's Feast* (1892), *The Angel of Death*, *The Ice Palace* (1900), music to Euripides' *Iphigenia in Aulis* and *The Trojan Women*, the ballet *The Magic Glass* (1902), a *Symphonie Lyrique*, a *Barcarolle*, an *Armenian Suite*, and *Musical Pictures* for orchestra, a Fantasia for piano and orchestra, a cantata (*Don Juan*), a string quartet, songs, pieces for piano, violin, violoncello, etc.

LIAPOUNOFF, SERGEI MICHAILOVITCH

Born at Jaroslav, November 30, 1859. Studied at Nijni-Novgorod, afterwards at the Moscow Conservatoire. He left the latter in 1883. Settled in Petrograd in 1885. In 1893 he embarked on a folksong collecting expedition in the Governments of Vologda, Viatka, and Kostroma; and from 1894 to 1902 acted as assistant director of the Imperial Chapel. His works include an orchestral *Ballade*, an *Overture Solennelle*, a symphony in B minor, two symphonic poems, two piano concertos, an *Ukrainian Rhapsody* for piano and orchestra, many piano pieces (including twelve *Etudes d'exécution transcendente*), several songs, etc. He edited the correspondence between Balakireff and Tchaïkovsky.

MEDTNER, NICOLAI
Born in Moscow, December 24, 1879, of German parents. He entered the Conservatoire there in 1891, studying under Safonoff. He left the Conservatoire in 1900, won the Rubinstein prize for piano-playing, and toured Russia and Germany as a concert pianist; on his return to Moscow he became professor of the piano at the Conservatoire. His works are almost all for the piano: they include three sonatas, a *Sonate-Ballade*, and a *Sonaten-Triade*. In addition he has published a sonata for violin and piano, *Three Nocturnes* for the same combination, and a number of striking songs. During the Great War he wrote a piano concerto, which is not yet published.

MOUSSORGSKY, MODEST PETROVITCH
Born at Karevo, in the Government of Pskov, March 29, 1839. He received a good training in singing and the piano as a boy at home; his studies were continued when, in 1849, he went to Petrograd to attend the Cadets' School, in preparation for a military career. In 1856 he was gazetted to the famous Preobrajensky regiment. In this and the next year he met Dargomijsky, Balakireff, and Borodine, and other members of the new Russian group, and set himself more seriously to the study of music. He left the army in 1861 to devote himself to the art, but he soon had to accept a small government post that hardly sufficed to keep him from utter poverty. After various tentative efforts, he entered the operatic field with *Boris Godounoff* (produced in Petrograd in 1874). This was followed by *Khovantchina*, which was left unfinished at the composer's death, completed and orchestrated by Rimsky-Korsakoff, and first performed in its entirety in 1885. Moussorgsky died in Petrograd, March 28, 1881.

His other works include the unfinished operas *The Matchmaker* (Gogol), *Salammbo* (Flaubert), a few orchestral works (*Intermezzo in modo classico*, a *Scherzo*, a *Turkish March*, and *Night on the Bare Mountain*), and many remarkable songs, the piano pieces *Pictures from an Exhibition*, etc.

MODERN RUSSIAN SONGS
VOLUME I

SPRING

(Original Key)

Translated from the Russian
of A. FET
by Frederick H. Martens

ACHILLES ALPHERAKY, Op. 16, Nº 1
(1846 -)

mp
cresc.
loam.
The vales are green with bud - ding
p cresc.
mp
cresc.
grass - - es, On ev- - 'ry bush the dew-pearls
dim.
p cresc.
mf
glow, Bird - songs ring clear as spring-time pass - es, The
dim.
cresc.
f
cloud - chain cracks at light - ning's blow. A -
f

gain, a - gain my heart - beats time their
cresc
dim.
dim.
poco mosso e cresc.
meas - ure To sounds that speak of home, As the
cresc.
blos - soms of spring - tide deck the loam.
ff

THE BOUQUET

(Composed in 1892)

(*Original Key*)

Translated from the Russian of VELICHKO (after Hafiz) by Constance Purdy

ACHILLES ALPHERAKY, Op.16, Nº5
1846-

splen - dor They dared to ri - - val you when
hom - age they should ren - der. The cul - - - prits
bound to - geth - er At your feet I lay!
f
cresc.
mf
pesante
ff
p
cresc.
rall.
dim.

WHEN NOCTURNAL SHADOWS GLIDING

THE SONG OF SONGS

Translated from a Russian paraphrase of "The Song of Solomon" Chap. III by Frederick H. Martens

(Original Key)

ACHILLES ALPHERAKY, Op. 21, №1 (1846-)

Ah, I find him not whose pow - - - er And whose
man - ly strength and beau - ty Fill my ar - dent soul with yearn - ing.
recitando
I sought my love and found him not, and sought a -
gain, I call'd his name un - ceas - ing, yet I call'd in
sf

vain...
sf
p
p
From my couch I rose, the cit-y slum-ber-bound and si-lent rest-ing: And by
p
long-ing torn I wan-der'd, tho' how vain my ut-most quest-ing. Oh, did

no one see my lov - er, — nor his way dis - cov - er?

f

Watch - men, has he pass'd your por - tals, the fair - est of all

mor - tals? O'er all the world I've sought him who my love did

gain, I've sought him, call'd up - on his name, yet all in vain.

cresc.
f
f
I will find my love, though in my
mf
search The grave a - lone re - quite me; Since nor fear nor doubt af -
fright me. And once found the pow - er burn - ing Of my kiss his free - dom

earn - ing, Then with me he'll be re - turn - ing.
f
I had sought my lov - er, had call'd him, all in
f
ad lib.
vain! Yet now have found him, nev - er - more to part a - gain!

WHEN LEAVES ARE FALLING SERE

Translated from the Russian of A. UMANETZ by Frederick H. Martens

(Original Key)

ACHILLES ALPHERAKY, Op. 26, No 3 (1846-)

flow - ers grow in rich and fra - grant bloom,
The flow'rs my heart bade germ - i - nate In all their ra - diant
beau - ty.
f
Ah, pluck, ah,

pluck those flow - ers grow - ing on my qui - et grave! With
them your dear blonde head a - dorn, be - lov - ed! They are
bear - ing, are bring - ing you the song that fills my soul. They
cresc.
bear the word - less mes - sage of my love.
f
cresc.
f
ff
mf

To V P Damaev

ALL THE BELLS, THE LITTLE BELLS

(Original Key)

Translated from the Russian of CKITALTZ by Constance Purdy

M. BAGRINOFSKI

near,
Down the sil - ver dust is pour -
- ing all a - round.
Not a star is seen in
heav - en's blue a - light,
On - ly
sfz
sfz
f
f
f
accelerando
p
pp colla parte
pp
p
8

myr - - - iad fires that spar - kle high in

f

air As the ring - - ing sounds all

pp *f marcato*

crim - - son in the night, In the heart is naught of

f

ff

trou - - ble or of care.

ff

slightly slower (♩ = 104)
Ah! Fly, thou my soul! Sur-ren - - - der thou to
poco
poco
dreams Ban-ish dis-mal fa-ces in the mer - - ry
dance.
Singing, tenderly
Eyes be - lov - ed in the dark-ness send their
beams. Vel - vet black the lash-es out from which they

Not quickly (♩=80)

p

glance. Night a-

riten.

p

p

round us has wrapp'd soft her vel-vet

cloak. Stars are hid - ing, and their

p

riten

lunga

light no long - er bring. But the

lunga

riten.

Tempo I

lit - - tle bells up - on the hor - ses' yoke Ev-er

of my love are chat-t'ring as they sing.

Joyously, very quickly (♩=132)

Ah! how

f

poco riten.

f

gai - - ly in the night the bells ring clear, And a

f

sim - - ple tale are tell - ing in their sound.
Swift the troi - ka, snow - lumps fly - ing far and
sfz
p
near, Down the sil - ver dust is
pour - ing all a - round.
sfff
colla canto

DEEP HIDDEN IN MY HEART
(IN MEINEM HERZCHEN)

Gr. A. GOLENISTSCHEFF KUTUSOFF
English translation by Constance Purdy
German translation by G. Löwenthal

(*Original Key, D*)

ANTON ARENSKY, Op. 44, № 6

p
mf
yet she the thresh-old pass'd, And fas - ten'd close the door,
schlich sie sich heim - lich ein, schloss hin - ter sich die Thür
p
p
pp
in shel - ter there a - bid - ing.
und weicht nicht mehr von hin - nen.
pp
p
pp
p
cresc.
ten.
Since then, when - e'er my soul is fill'd with doubt and fear
Seit - dem, wenn mein Ge - müth, von All tags - sor - gen schwer,
p
mp
cresc.
ten.
That by their wan - ton sport sink hap - pi - ness and rea - son,
Die eig' - ne Zwei - fel - sucht kein Glücks - ge - fühl lässt blei - ben,
mp

f accelerando
And when my spir - it worn is cir-cled round by night
kein Hoff-nungs-strahl er - hellt das Dun-kel rings um - her
mf accelerando
mp
poco ritardando
And life a ra - ging storm seems full of bit - ter trea - son;
und mir den Sinn be - fängt des lau - ten Ta - ges Trei - ben
p
poco ritardando
a tempo pp
Then all at once I hear a sooth -
ver - neh - me plötz - lich ich gar wun -
a tempo
pp
mp
p
- ing mel - o - dy, My guest so won - der-ful
- der sü - ssen Sang: die Klaus - ne-rin in mir
f
mf

is con - so - la - tion bring - ing.
singt mir von Glück und Won - ne.
p
Once more
Ich fühl'
p
p
to joy I wake...
mich neu - be - lebt,
mf
the storm clouds roll - ing back, We
es weicht die Sor - ge bang dem
mp
f
ritard.
lis - ten to my cap - tive, in the still - ness sing - ing.
Sang der Zau - be - rin, wie Ne - bel von der Son - ne.
ritard.
mf
p a tempo
rit.
pp
ppp
Ped.

REVERY
(IM HALBSCHLAF)

(Original Key)

Translated from the Russian
of L. MUNSCHTEIN by Constance Purdy
German version by Lena Esbeer

ANTON ARENSKY, Op. 60, № 3
(1862-1906)

mf
spring my au - tumn days.
Herb - stes - ta - ge Rest.
p
And dark and pen - sive eyes are
Wie freund - lich lä - cheln mir die
mf
look-ing at me kind - ly,
träu-me - ri-schen Bli - cke.
cresc.
Sweet words of love I in the eve-ning still-ness reap;
manch Lie - bes-wort durch-dringt die a - bend - li - che Ruh.
f
Un - real tho' these may be as fair - y tales of child - hood,
Und sind es Mär - chen nur von still er - sehn - tem Glü - cke,
f
p
I love to hear them while I'm dream - ing half a - sleep.
so hört in hal - bem Traum sich's ih - nen woh - lig zu.
mf ritenuto
p
ritenuto

SONG OF THE LITTLE FISH
(FISCHLEINS LIED)

Translated from the Russian
of M. LERMONTOFF
by Robert H. Hamilton
German version by Lina Esbeer

(Original Key)

ANTON ARENSKY, Op. 27, № 1
(1862-1906)

wild, In cool - ness rests the
hier; So kükl ist's, so voll
mf
mf
p
sea.
Ruh'.
8
dim.
mf
My mer - ry sis - ters call thee here, All cir - cling
Die Schwe - stern ru - fe ich her - bei, Wir schwin - gen
mf
in the dance, Thy wear - y, care - worn
uns im Tanz, Bis dei - ne mü - de
mf

rit.
a tempo
soul we'll cheer, And calm thy trou - bled glance.
See - le frei, Dein Au - ge vol - ler Glanz.
rit.
p
a tempo
dim.
p
pp
O stay, my child,
O blei - be hier,
cresc.
cresc.
mf
And lin - ger here by me!
Du hol - der Kna - be mein!
mf
pp
Here
Ruh'
pp

sleep, thy veil as clear as glass, Thy couch like
aus, dein Pfühl ist ja so weich, Die De - cke
moon - beams bright; The years will come and
licht und klar; Schnell flicht die Zeit in
a - ges pass 'Neath spell of dreams' de - light.
mei - nem Reich Du träumst, wirst's nicht ge - wahr.
O, treas - ure
O, trau - ter

mine, my love to thee In
Schatz, ich hehl' es nicht, Ich
full - - - est por - - - tion see
lie - - - be dich so sehr
My love is like the o-cean
Wie mei - - - nes Le - - bens Freud' und
free, 'Tis all my
Licht, Mein frei - es
mf
dim.
mf
dim.
pp
pp

ML-2840-6

ten
mf
life to me, O
Wel - - len-meer. Mein
mf
cresc.
treas - - ure mine, O treas - - - ure
trau - - ter Schatz, mein trau - - - ter
cresc.
f
p
mine, O tar - ry here with me!
Schatz, o blei - be hier bei mir!
f
p
mf
dimin.
p
pp
ppp

THE EAGLE
(DER ADLER)

(Original Key, D♭)

Translated from the Russian
of Count GOLENISTSCHEFF-KUTUSOFF
by Frederick H Martens
German version by G. Lowenthal

ANTON ARENSKY, Op.44, Nº 1
(1862-1906)

Adagio

PIANO

mf

f dim. *mp dim.* *p*

p

An ea-gle poised on crag-gy
Ein Ad-ler sass auf Fels-ge-

peak, His vis-ion lost in space sur-round-ing___ Like
stein, den Blick ge-rich-tet in die Wei-te,___ dem

mf

pil-grim lone, whose mind a-far___ The un-known deeps of thought is
Pil-ger gleich, der ganz al-lein___ tief-ern-stem Sin-nen wird zur

mf dim. *p dim.* *p*

sound - ing. The cir-cling swarm of less-er birds Noi-si - ly
Beu - te. Der an-dern Vö-gel lau-ter Chor um-schwär-mte

clam-or,'neath him swirl-ing; The dust of earth the wan - ton
ihn mit Schrei'n und Sin - gen; im Wir - - bel - wind zu ihm em-

winds Up to his ee - - rie high are
por, ver - sucht' der Er - - den-staub zu

whirl - - ing.
drin - - gen.

di - mi - nu -

p
He scorns the birds' dis-cor-dant cries, The whirl-wind's
Doch schien er nicht die Vo-gel schaar, noch auch den
-en- -do
p
mf
di-
fu-rious rage dis - dain - ing, — A - loof, the mas-ter of the
Wir-bel - wind zu hö - ren, — es liess der kö-nig-li-che
mi- -nu- -en- -do
skies Still holds the dream past their at - tain - ing.
Aar in sei-nem Sin-nen sich nicht stö - ren
Più mosso
mp
cre-
E-nough of dream-ing! But a glance At earth's poor
Ge-nug des Sin-nens! Ei-nen Blick des Er-den-
cre-
3

-scen - do
mf
f
triv - ial do - ings deign - - ing. He turns to heav'n's blue dome a-
trei - bens nicht' - gen Din - - gen, dann kehrt zur Hö - - he er zu-
-scen - do
mf
f
rit.
gain, His might - y pin - ions up - ward strain - ing.
rück, aus-brei - tend die ge - walt' - gen Schwin-gen.
rit.
Tempo I
p
cresc.
Home, where is raised his fa - ther's throne, O'er sun and
Heim - wärts zu sei - ner Vä - ter Thron, be - nach - bart
pp
cresc.
moon and stars e - rect - - - ed, The
Son - - - - nen, Mond und Ster - - - - nen, nahm

Più mosso
mf
roy - - al ea - gle cleaves the air, To dim ho - -
sei - - nen Flug der Kö - nigs-sohn zum Wol - ken - -
mf
ri - - - zons, cloud - re - flect - - - - - - -
saum, zu blau - en Fern - - - - - -
8
mf
ed. The dust of earth, its bau - bles
nen. Und Er - den - staub und Er - den -

light, His up-ward flight leaves far be - hind him, No
tand hat bald er hin - ter sich ge - las - sen, und
chains of hate or love may bind — him, In az - ure
un - be-rührt von Lieb' und Has - sen, im blau - en
rit.
p
pp
deeps — he fades from sight.
Ae - ther er ent - schwand.
a tempo
mp a tempo
L.H.

BURNING OUT IS THE SUNSET'S RED FLAME

(Original Key, F♯)

Translated from the Russian of V KULCHINSKY by Constance Purdy

MILI BALAKIREFF (1837-1910)

forth now her claim, Si-lence falls o - ver
for - est and mead - ow.
p
O for - get thou, my heart, all those days, Days re -
p
bel - lious, in-spired and soul-free-ing. My poor heart, seek the sleep which al-lays!

mf
My poor heart, seek the sleep which al-lays! Call not
f
back ___ those dear hours in-to be-ing!
p
From the
clouds comes the moon's gen-tle light, Sil-ver

flood - - ed the fields soft - ly glit - ter,
Why, O
f
why can she not by her might
Heal the
f
wounds of my soul, deep and bit - - ter?
pp
perdendosi
ppp
poco rit.

THE PINE-TREE
(DER FICHTENBAUM)

(Original Key)

Translated from the Russian
of LERMONTOFF by Constance Purdy
German version by Lina Esbeer

MILI BALAKIREFF
(1837-1910)

Allegretto agitato

p

His gaze turns in dreams to the far - a - way
Der Träu - men - de sieht die ver - schmach - ten - den

tremolo

sf *p*

des - ert, That land of the morn's ra - diant skies, Where
Hal - me Der Wü - ste, die end - los, sich dehnt, Wo

f *p*

Commodo

lone - ly and sad, by a burnt cliff - side lean - ing, A
ein - sam und trau - rig die herr - lich - ste Pal - me An

parlando

Tempo I

beau - ti - ful palm vain - ly sighs.
glü - hen - der, Fel - sen - wand lehnt.

poco riten.

pp

NOCTURNE
(NACHTSTÜCK)

(Original Key)

Translated from the Russian
by Frederick H. Martens

MILI BALAKIREFF
(1837 - 1910)

might this fair mo - ment stay__ What rap - ture! The
von euch um - ge - ben zu sein__ Wie won - nig! Wie
Listesso tempo
wave, ah, how fair and the steppe how__ wide, How
schön ist die Wo - ge, die Step - pe so weit, Wie
Listesso tempo
charm - ing the Spring in the dress of a bride, We're__ find - ing; How
schön in des Len - zes bunt schim-mern-dem Kleid Die__ Blu - me; Wie
poco a poco agitato e crescendo
ra - diant, ex - alt - ed, is love's glow - ing light, How
hehr ist der Lie - be hell - glän - zen - des Licht, Wie
poco a poco agitato e crescendo

grate - ful the joys that true friend - ship re - quite The
hehr treu - e Freund - schaft so lieb - reich und schlicht, Be -
f passionato
crown grate - ful hearts e'er for glo - ry by right Are
glu - ckend der Kranz, den die Dank - bar - keit flicht Dem
f passionato
wind - ing!
Ruh - me!
di - mi - nu - en -
poco ritenuto
do
p pp
Tempo I
Tempo I
p
pp
I gazed on the skies, Ves - ta
Ich blick - te zum Him - mel, die

glow'd on high; O'er spa - ces un-bound-ed the glance of my eye Might
Ves - te glänzt; Es schwei - fet das Au - ge um - her un-be-grenzt Hoch
wan - der.
o - - ben.
The
Die
stars spar-kled clear like an o - cean of flame, The mem - 'ries of child - hood, they
Ster - ne, sie glüh - ten ein Flam - men-meer schier Er - in - n'rung der Kind - heit er -
call'd me by name, And then I thought:
wach - te in mir. Da dach - - te ich:

earth has no joy such as that up yon - der!
bes - ser wohl ist es als hier Da dro - ben!
L.H.
No joy like
Bes - ser ist
that up yon - der!
es da dro - ben!

THE FAIR GARDEN

ROMANCE

(Original Key, Db)

Translated from the Russian
by Constance Purdy

ALEXANDER BORODINE
(1834-1887)

pp
cresc.
dise Whose green walks and e'er - chan - ging path - ways
cresc.
dim. e rall.
p calando
dim. e rall.
Lead thro' deep, sweet - smell - ing thick - ets and bow'rs To slim
dim. e rall.
dim. e rall.
pp
reeds fill'd with nests.
pp
più animato e molto espressivo
p cresc.
Oh, hap - py, hap - py ye, hav - ing for
p cresc.

mf appassionato
sov - 'reign dear A la - dy fair in spir - it kind,
mf
maestoso
rall e dim.
Whose fa - mous coat of arms
sempre dim.
O - ver the pal - ace
rall. e dim.
por - tal is bla - zon'd on high.
ppp
rit.
pp
p
Ped.

To Modest P. Moussorgsky

A DISSONANCE

ROMANCE

(Original Key)

English version by
Frederick H. Martens

ALEXANDER BORODINE
(1834 - 1887)

mf
while A dis - so-nance, you re - veal it In
mf
f
ff
rall.
voice and in glance, and in smile! You know, nor may you con -
rall
f
ff
p
ceal it!

MY SONGS ARE ENVENOMED AND BITTER

(MON CHANT EST AMER ET SAUVAGE)

(Original Key, in E♭)

French version (after HEINE)
by Paul Collin
English version by Charles Fonteyn Manney

ALEXANDER BORODINE
(1834 - 1887)

The composer used a free metrical version in Russian of Heine's poem, which makes the retention of the German original impossible.

rall.
a tempo p
rall.
My songs are en - ven - om'd and bit - ter, Yet how could they oth - er-wise
Mon chant est a - mer et sau-va - ge, com - ment pour - rait - il ê - tre
rall.
a tempo
rall.
f
p
cresc.
f
a tempo
be? A ser - pent I bear in my heart, In the heart that is
doux? Je porte un ser-pent dans mon coeur, dans ce coeur que rem -
f
a tempo
dim.
fill'd, love, with thee.
plit ton a - mour.
mf
f
p

THE SEA
(LA MER)
(Original Key)

Translated by Grace Hall
French version by Paul Collin

ALEXANDER BORODINE
(1834-1887)

p
waves.
rie.
Brav - ing the
Sur son na -
p
cre - scen do
f
threat of the swift sur - ging tide in its an - ger.
vire, et des vents af - fron - tant la co - lè - re,
cre - scen - do
f
dim.
p
The ma - ri - ner steers his frail bark mid the
s'a - van - ce par - mi les é - cueils un ma -
p
f
rocks and the dan - ger.
rin té - mé - rai - re.
The
La
f
dim.

Più animato
deep with its salt spray his pale face is
bri - se si - nis - tre an - non - ce - lo -
mf
cresc.
f
lash-ing, It her - alds the
ra - ge, la vague é - cu -
dim.
mf
tem - pest with pon-der-ous crash-ing,
meu - se lui crache au vi - sa - ge
f
di - mi - nu - en - do
rallentando

p meno mosso
The while in his spir-it like
C'est vers son pa - ys que l'em-
meno mosso
Ped
bea-cons are burn - ing Vis-ions of home and the hope of re - turn-ing,
por - te son rê - ve, et plein de joie l'heu-re lui sem - ble brè - ve;
Vis-ions of joy and sweet vis ions of lov - ing, Fair past be-
à ses cô - tés u - ne fem - me qu'il ai - me, bon - - heur su-
più mosso e animato
liev - ing. He dreams on, a - bout him the waves roar and thun-der, His
prê - - me, le des - tin lui fait un sort di - gne d'en - vi - e, à
cresc.

heart is at peace, full of joy and of won-der, For love soon will crown hap-py
tout es-pé-rer l'a-ve-nir le con-vi-e, l'a-mour ra-di-eux va bril-
dim.
days with-out num-ber.
ler sur sa vi-e.
pp
cresc. e accel.
f
Tempo I
rall.
a tempo
p

The sea
La mer
cresc.
toss - - es and raves,
gronde et mu - git,
f
p
While fling - ing
rou - lant ses
cresc.
heav'n - - ward its waves.
flots en fu - rie,
f

Stead-fast - ly steer - ing, the ma - ri - ner
fier et vail - lant le ma - rin veut aux
p
cresc.
stands by the rud - der;
flots te - nir tê - te.
f
p
With
Il
cour - age un - fail - ing he smiles where one wis - er might
lutte, il com - bat, il s'a - charne à dompt - er la tem -
cresc.
shud - der.
pê - te
f
p
The
La

bil - lows shout ven - geance, they laugh in his
vague é - cu - meu - se lui crache au vi -
mf
cresc.
f
face; With death for op -
sa - ge, il pous - se la
dim.
mf
po - nent how win the race?
bar - que loin du ri - va - ge
cresc.
f
dim.
rall.
fp

p
più animato cresc.
A - gain and a - gain for the o - pen he
Il lut - te sans trève et re - dou - ble d'ef -
più animato cresc.
f
steers, A - gain and a - gain back to land -
fort, la va - gue sans trè - ve l'é - loi -
f
ward he veers,
gne du port.
ff
rall. e dim.

Tempo I
Till, toss'd at ran - - - - dom, the
Et bal - lot - té - - - - e au
Tempo I
sport of the blast
gré de la mer
A - gainst the rocks he
la bar - - - que som - - bre
dash - - es at last.
au gouffre a - mer.

p poco a poco
No
Et
poco a poco
cresc.
sign re - mains of man, boat or
main - te - nant plus rien sur les
cresc.
sail, The wind sweeps the main
flots, dans l'om - - bre le vent
with its des - - o - late wail.
fait un bruit de san - glots.
ff
ff

fp
p
pp

To Nickolas Rimsky-Korsakoff

THE SLEEPING PRINCESS
(LA PRINCESSE ENDORMIE)

Translated from the Russian
by Constance Purdy
French version by Grandmoussin

BALLADE
(Original Key, A♭)

Words and Music by
ALEXANDER BORODINE
(1834-1887)

sleeps!
dort!
mf
dim.
rall. pp
Più mosso
All at once the for-est qui-et Wakes to laugh-ter wild and ri-ot;
Mais sou-dain dans l'ombre é-paisse é-cla-tent des cris et des ri-res;
cresc.
Witch-es, sat-yrs nois-y swarm Round the maid-en's sleep-ing form.
les es-prits des bois pas-sent en ron-de sans rom-pre ce som-meil.
f
dim.
rall p
pp
rall.

Tempo I
Ev - er, in the for - est deep, That en - chant - ed, death-like sleep!
Sans cou - leur, com - me la mort, La prin - ces - se tou - jours dort!
She sleeps!
dort! dort!
mf
Più animato
p
cresc. poco a poco
Le - gends say that to her bow - er There will come a prince, whose pow - er
On di - sait qu'en la fo - rêt un jour vien-drait un preux, un che - va -
p marcato
cresc. poco a poco

f
Will the mag - ic charm dis - pel, And the prin - cess wake, to dwell
lier sans peur, au coeur fi - de - le, pour sau - ver en - fin la bel - le,
f
Free for ev - er from the spell, the fa - - - - tal
et sou - dain bri - ser l'en - chan - te ment fa -
rall.
spell!
tal!
più lento
p
One by
Mais les
dim.

one the days are go - ing, In - to years and cy - cles
jours s'én vont sans trè - ve, Le temps pas - se comme un
p
grow - ing; Still there comes of life no sound; All is
re - ve, Et ja - mais nul n'ap - pa - raît Dans la
wrapt in sleep pro-found!
nuit de la fo - rêt!
Tempo I
p
So with - in the
La prin - cesse aux
for - est deep Lies the prin - cess fast a - sleep.
si doux yeux, Au re - pos mys - té - ri - eux,

Seal'd her eyes in ma - gic slum - ber, She, thro' days that
Par le char - me d'u - ne fé - e Au som - meil est
none can num - ber, Sleeps, sleeps!
con - dam - née, Et dort! dort!
mf
pp
And no liv - ing soul can tell When she'll wa - ken from the
Quel fa - tal et mor - ne som - meil! Quand son - ne - ra l'heu - re du ré -
pp
spell.
veil?
mf
p
pp

WHEN GAZING IN THINE EYES
(WENN ICH IN DEINE AUGEN SEH')

HEINRICH HEINE*) (1799-1856)
Translated by Arthur Westbrook

J. BLEICHMANN, Op.8, No 4

*) The music was composed to a Russian version of Heine's poem

pp
dream of heav'n could be more blest:
ü - ber mich wie Him - mels - lust;
pp
pp quasi parlando
But when thou say'st: "I love but thee!" I fall to weep - - ing,
doch wenn du sprichst: ich lie - be dich! so muss ich wei - - nen,
pp
weep - - ing bit - ter - ly
wei - - nen bit - ter - lich.
col canto
a tempo
p
morendo

AH, IF MOTHER VOLGA
(ACH, WENN MUTTER WOLGA)

(Original Key)

Translated from the Russian of Count A. TOLSTOI by Constance Purdy
German version by Lina Esber

CÉSAR CUI, Op. 67
(1835-1918)

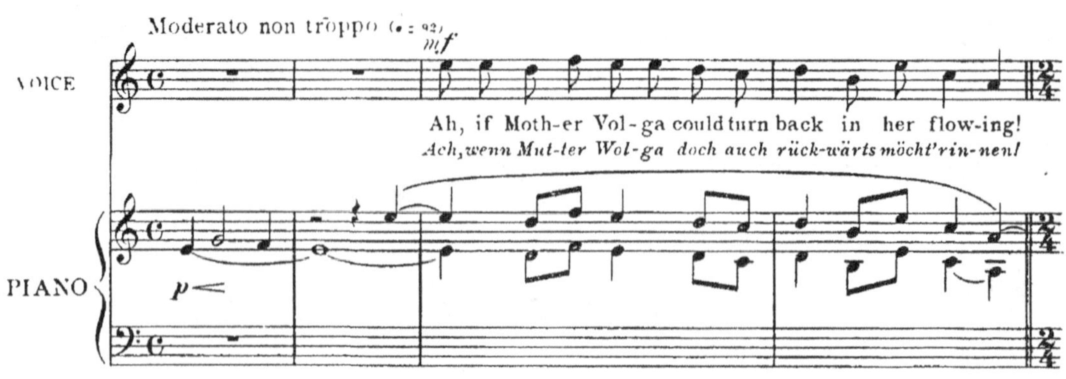

f
faith - ful and un - end - ing!
und auch Treu - e hal - ten!
If the o - cean's depths we, my
Könn - ten wir die Tie - fen des
mf
broth - ers, could meas - ure!
Mee - res er - schau - en
If a maid - en's beau - ty
und den sü - ssen Re - den
trust as well as treas - - ure!
schö - ner Mäd - chen trau - - en!

mf
Ah, could each old wife be youth-ful as her daugh - ter!
Ach, wenn al - le Wei - - ber jun - ge Weib-lein wä - ren!
p
If were in the wine - flask a lit - tle less wa - ter!
Man sein Flasch-chen Brannt - wein ver - dünnt nicht müsst' le - ren!
If to seek our lips were but the gob-let's mis - sion!
Wenn der vol - le Be - cher ständ' den Lip-pen nä - her.
f
Could the dev - il take all ty - rants to per - di - tion!
Wenn der Teu - fel hol - te al - le Rechts-ver - dre - her!
LH
mf

mf

If with - in our pock - ets gold might jin - gle ev - er!

Wenn die Ta - schen klan - gen stets ge - füllt mit Gol - de!

R.H.

p

And if each man of us might a coat lack nev - er!

Wenn den Rock man tra - gen durf - te den man woll - te!

poco rit.

p *Pochissimo meno mosso*

If each day the hun - gry might be nour - ish'd du - ly! And

Wenn der Hun - ger - lei - der nim - mer hun - gern müss - te und

mf

if Fa - ther Czar could but know all things tru - - ly!

Va - ter - chen Zar — die Wahr - heit stets wiss - - te!

f

mf

To Valentine Constantinovna Lind ff

DUSK FALLEN

Translated from the Russian
by Constance Purdy

Original Key, F♯

CESAR CUI
(1835-1918)

p
rit.
Thy smile was as of yore, I loved it, oh, how dear - ly, Thy soft - ly wov - en braids held
a tempo
p
once a-gain their pow'r; Thy som-bre eyes re-flecting all their old-time sad - ness,
pp
poco riten.
mf
a tempo
Look'd in - to mine once more at eve - ning's qui - et hour, at
colla voce
riten.
pp poco più mosso
eve - ning's qui - et hour.
pp

HUNGER SONG
(DAS HUNGERLIED)

Original Key

Translated from the Russian
of N. NEKRASOFF
by Deems Taylor

CÉSAR CUI
(1835-1918)

His ash - en face is gaunt and worn; How glazed and dim his fail - ing eyes.
Er selbst ist fahl, sein Blick ist leer, als ob er stets im Rau - sche wär'
He walks, he crawls. He moans, he sighs. And now be - holds the rus-tling
Er geht im Schlaf. er keucht, und kriecht da-hin wo sich sein Rog-gen
corn! He stops and stares with hun - gry eyes, He sways,
wiegt. Dort steht er wie ein Göt - zen-bild und singt —
and fall - ing, faint - ly cries: "O corn, put forth
kein Laut der Brust ent-quillt: „Ge - deih', ge - deih'
mf
p

thy ri-pen'd ear! Be-hold, thy son lies
mein Rog-gen-feld!. Ich bin's, der dich mit
starv-ing here!
Müh be-stellt.
ac- -cel- -er- -an- -do
A might-y sheaf of corn I'll take,
Wird schwer dein Brod wie mei-ne Noth,
A might-y loaf of bread I'll bake.
und wird es bit-te-rer als Tod,
mf
poco
'Tis mine to eat, All mine to eat,
ich geb's nicht her, ver-zehr's al-lein,
a poco
Though son and moth-er starve....
ob Sohn, ob Mut-ter fleht,
f
'Tis mine!"
'sbleibt mein!"
p
ff

O THOU ROSE-MAIDEN

Translated from the Russian
of A. PUSHKIN
by Constance Purdy

(Original Key)

ALEXANDER DARGOMIJSKY
(1813 - 1869)

The night-in - gale— with - in the lau - - rel,
Of wood-land song - sters— feath - er'd king,
Near that proud— flow-er of rare— beau-ty,
slowly dim.
The rose so haugh - - ty of rare beau - - ty,
slowly dim

a tempo
In sweet-est thrall-dom spends his days, In sweet - - est
a tempo
sf
thrall - - dom spends his days,
p
And soft - - ly sings to her his lays,
p
And soft - - ly sings to her his lays,

And soft - - - - - ly
marcato
marcato
sings to her, and soft - - ly to
her sings his lays!
rit.
dim.
p rit.
pp a tempo

AH, TWINE NO BLOSSOMS

(O, WINDE KEINE DUFT'GE BLÜTE)

Translated from the Russian of D. RATHAUS by Deems Taylor
German version by Lina Esbeer

(Original Key)

REINHOLD GLIÈRE, Op. 18, Nº 7
(1875 -)

go.
ganz
dim.
mf
Ah, come no more to smile up - on me... That
O, dass ich nie dein Lä - cheln schau - te, nie
mf
lim - pid smile so long for - got, My heart's de -
hör - te was dein Mund ver - spricht, mein zar - tes
p
p
sire, my own be - lov - ed... Dost thou not hear?
Kind, du hol - de Trau - te, dich wie - der lie -
cresc.
f
f

*) English text only

f
Wast - - - - ed my soul with bit - ter long - -
Was kann die See - le dir ge - wäh - -
- ing: What now re - mains to give to thee?
- ren die nur von her - bem Lei - de zehrt.
dim.
p
f
dim.
p

THE JOURNEY

(Composed in 1840)

(Original Key, D)

English version by Constance Purdy

MICHAIL IVANOVITCH GLINKA
(1804-1857)

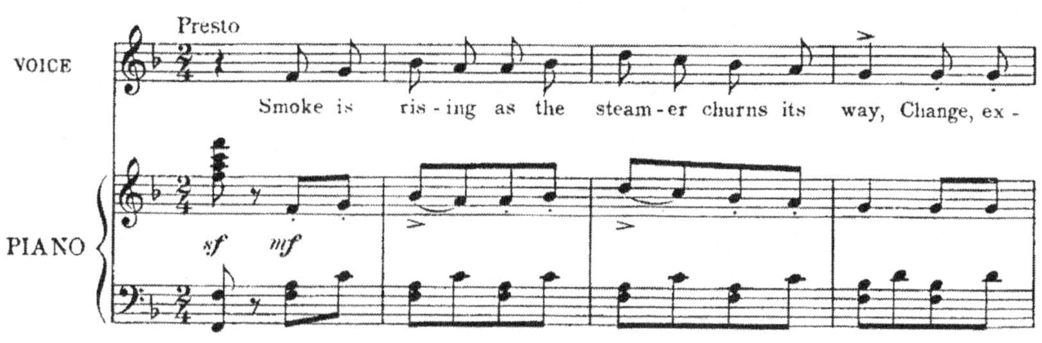

rid-ing goes the train thro' mead-ows glid - ing. Smoke is ris-ing as the
steam-er churns its way! Change, ex - cite-ment un-a - bat-ing, fun, im-
pa-tience, ea-ger wait-ing, Crowds of peo-ple all on pleas-ure bent are gay,
Crowds of peo-ple all on pleas-ure bent are gay. Fast and
sf
f
p accel.

fast - er ev - er rid - ing goes the train thro' mead - ows glid - - - -
ing, Fast and fast - er ev - er rid - ing goes the train thro' mead-ows
mf
con tutta forza
glid - - - - - ing, Thro' the mead - - ows swift - ly
glid - ing, swift - ly glid - - - - - - - - - -
ff

con grazia ed espressione ma leggiero
ing.
1. Yet swift - er by
2. But sun - shine and
p staccato il basso
far do our thoughts_ se - cret fly,___ The heart keep - ing
ver - dure ne'er suf - f'ring_re - call;___ And yon - der clear
count_ as the mo - ments go by; Their deep sub - tle
nights_cast their flame_ o - ver all; Each mo - - ment of
gleam on the way_ far ex - tend - ing; You mur - mur: "The
meet - ing with bliss_ o - ver - flow - ing; On hours, e'en of

D.C.
time oft, O Lord, seems un - end - ing!"
part - - ing, hope's sweet - ness be - stow - ing.
D.C.
Tempo I
Smoke is ris - ing as the steam - er churns its way! Change, ex -
sf
mf
cite - ment un - a - bat - ing, fun, im - pa - tience, ea - ger wait - ing: Crowds of
sf
peo - ple all on pleas - ure bent are gay, Fast and fast - er ev - er

rid-ing goes the train thro' mead-ows glid-ing. Smoke is ris-ing as the
steam-er churns its way! Change, ex-cite-ment un-a-bat-ing, fun, im-
pa-tience, ea-ger wait-ing! Crowds of peo-ple all on pleas-ure bent are
gay, Crowds of peo-ple all on pleas-ure bent are gay

p accel
Fast and fast-er ev-er rid-ing goes the train thro' mead-ows glid-
p accel
-ing, Fast and fast-er ev-er rid-ing goes the train thro' mead-ows
mf
con tutta forza
glid-ing, Thro' the mead-ows swift-ly glid-
ing, swift-ly glid-ing.
ff
sf
sf

STAR OF THE NORTH

(Original Key)

Translated from the Russian of ROSTOPCHINE by Constance Purdy

MICHAIL IVANOVITCH GLINKA (1804-1857)

forth; For a bride dwells there-in, fair-est, sweet - - est_ of_

all, Of all stars most re - splen - dent, the star_____ of_ the

north. Deep ab - sorb'd doth she brood and sad her thoughts,_ On the

cir - clet of gold, her wed-ding-ring, great_ tears from her

eyes hot and heav - y fall!
Of her dear one
is she think - ing night and day.
He, her hus - band, has gone to a far dis - tant

land, And to her may not soon, may not soon come a - gain. He will come back a - gain when the spring - time shall reign, With God's sun - light on high then shall joy hold sway.

ON THE STEPPE
(TRISTE EST LE STEPPE)

(Original Key)

Translated from the Russian
of PLESTCHEIEFF by Charles Fonteyn Manney
French version by M. D. Calvocoressi

ALEXANDER GRETCHANINOFF, Op. 5, Nº1
(1864)

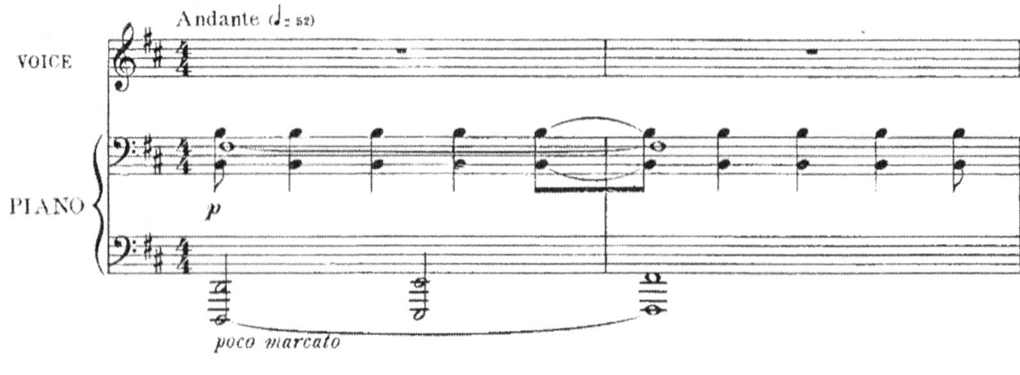

Nev - er a flow'r smiles to glad-den me, Nev - er a bird sings its
Point d'ar-bres verts ni de frais buis-sons pour a-bri-ter les oi-
sempre p
lay. Down drops the night on its sa-ble wing,
seaux Lu - gu - bre - ment tombe un soir obs - cur,
lugubre
mf
Hid - ing each glim - mer-ing star: What sum-mons back to my
pas une é - toile au ciel noir: Je ne sais plus quels doux
poco stringendo
p
mf
poco stringendo e cresc.
mem - o - ry Vis - ions of you from a -
mots d'a - mour, pas un tel soir tu m'as

ff con libertà
far?
dit
Vis - ions of you, my be -
Par un tel soir, ô ma
dolce
ff
colla parte
mf
a tempo
lov - ed one,
bien - ai-mée!
mf
Smil - ing and fair as the morn;
Tu sou - ri - ais ten-dre - ment;
a tempo
p
p
Driv - ing the shad - ow - y night a - way,
je te re - vois et je crois sou - dain
pp
cresc.
tr
cresc. poco a poco
Light - ing my path - way for - lorn.
qu'il n'est plus d'ombre en ces lieux;
tr
poco
a
poco

ff
Now hear the song of the night - in-gale Thrill - ing the spa - ces on
les chants su - a - ves des ros - si - gnols mon - tent des bois par - fu -
tr
f
high; Flow'rs in the des - - ert are
més, au - tour de moi mil - le
p
dim.
pp
blos - som - ing, Stars deck with jew - els the
fleurs sont nées et tout le ciel res - plen-
molto rit.
a tempo
sky!
dit
mf
poco rit. e dim.
pp

PALM BRANCHES

(Original Key, C)

Translated from the Russian of A. BLOCK by Grace Hall

ALEXANDER GRETCHANINOFF, Op. 47, № 2
(1864-)

a tempo
way. Lust - y winds blow o'er the sky, Down the rain drops
a tempo
p
poco cresc.
poco rit.
from on high, Still the flames burn on.
a tempo
On this Feast of
poco rit.
più f
a tempo
mf
f
Palms To our Lord we sing our Psalms From the ear-ly break of dawn.
più rit.
f
mf
simile

SLUMBER REIGNS
(ALLES SCHLÄFT)

Translated from the Russian of A. FET by Frederick H. Martens
German version by S. König

(Original Key)

ALEXANDER GRETCHANINOFF
(1864 -)

None may lis - ten, save per -
Es be - lauscht uns viel - leicht
p subito
ff
haps the night - in - gale.
nur die Nach - ti - gall.
And she'll nev - er hear us,
A - ber sie hört uns nicht,
f
ff
her own song her pride,
ihr Lied is zu laut,
Hand to heart a - lone the se - cret shall con - fide
Nur die Hand es dem Her - zen heim - lich ver - traut,
p
f

That, u - nit - ed here, the high-est joys en - thrall,
Dass uns hier ver - ein - igt hoch-ster Er - den - gluck
p
f
That this mo - ment is bless-ed o - ver
Und wir se - lig sind in die - sem Au - gen -
ff
mf
all;
blick;
Trem - bling hands to heart the
Zit - ternd thei - let es die
dim
pp
tid - ings glad dis - close,
Hand dem Her - zen mit,
That an - oth - er heart as soft - ly stirs and
Dass in ihr die an - d're lei - se bebt und

glows. Then re - spond - ing to this
glüht, Wenn dies Be- - ben nun bis
p cresc.
si - lent sign of grace, Ar - dent, fond,
hin zum Her-zen steigt Lie - be - voll
ff
con liberta
a tempo
we are en - clasp'd in love's em - brace!
sich Schul - ter dann zu Schul-ter neigt.
colla parte
a tempo
mf
pp
p
ff
sf
sf

SNOWFLAKES
(SCHNEEFLÖCKCHEN)

Translated from the Russian of W. BRUSSOFF by Constance Purdy
German version by Lena Esber

(Original Key, D minor)

ALEXANDER GRETCHANINOFF, Op. 47, №1
(1864-)

rit.
you come dan - - - cing.
ab vom Him - - - mel.
rit.
a tempo
mf cresc.
simile
How can we with - stand you long - er! You are
Ge - gen euch sind wir die Schwa - chen, frei - e
a tempo
mf molto staccato e cresc.
free, in num - bers strong - er, At your will you can - en -
Flöck - chen, ihr könnt la - chen, könnt uns all' zu - sam - men
p
ff
fold us
fe - - gen,
ff

In your shroud of white and hold
Stadt und Land ins Bahr-tuch le-
ff
us
gen.
ff
mf
(rit.)
rit.
p a tempo
Snow-flakes fly-ing
We-het, weht ihr
a tempo
p
o'er our por-tals. Pit-y us poor mor-tals!
Flo-cken-ster-ne, uns nur bleibt hubsch fer-ne!

O you hosts of white ad-van-cing, Out of heav-en

Schnee-ge-stö-ber, Schnee-ge-wim-mel, streut uns Gott her-

you come dan- - - - cing.

ab vom Him- - - - mel.

1. (rit.)

rit.

2. rit.

a tempo

morendo

- - - - - cing.

- - - - - mel.

rit.

a tempo

smorzando

p

To J. A. Melinkoff

THE CAPTIVE
(LE CAPTIF)

Translated from the Russian
of PUSCHKIN by Grace Hall
French version by M. D. Calvocoressi

(Original Key)

ALEXANDER GRETCHANINOFF, Op.20, № 4
(1864-)

deep fel - low feel - ing I read in his eyes. He
tourne, il se po - se, puis ronge u - ne proie, et
f ma non troppo
brings to my grat - ing His still bleed - ing prey, He
puis il la quit - te, re - gar - de vers moi, un
p
non sostenendo
tears it and rends it In
rê - ve, le mê - me, nous
p misterioso e non sostenendo
porhissimo marcato
rit.
grim sav - age play. His
han - te tous deux. Son
rit.

a tempo *poco a poco cresc. ed acceler.*

eyes to mine speak - ing Seem clear - ly to say, In

cri per-çant mon - te, je lis dans ses yeux, j'

a tempo

p *poco a poco cresc. ed acceler.*

bold in - vi - ta - tion: "Now up and a - way! Ah,

sens qu'il m'im - plo - re: "Fu - yons loin d'i - ci! Nos

ff *sf* *sf*

Più largamente

ha - sten, my broth - er, A - rise, it is time! Thy

ai - les sont li - bres; viens, frère, il est temps! les

ff *mf*

heart, like mine own, Seeks some fair hap - pier clime. O'er

ci - mes sont blan - ches, l'a - zur nous at - tend, les

moun - tain and val - ley A - far let us
bri - ses ma - ri - nes, les clairs ho - ri -
p
poco a poco cresc.
fly, For lords of cre -
zons La - bas, dans l'es -
con libertà
rit.
ff acceler.
Molto più mosso
tion thou and
pa nous som les

ANOTHER LITTLE HOUR I BEGGED

(ICH WOLLT' EIN WENIG MIT DIR PLAUDERN)

Translated from the Russian of A PLESCHTSCHEJEFF by Constance Purdy
German version by S König

(Original Key)

ALEXANDER GRETCHANINOFF
(1864 -)

a tempo
rit.
near, — You dropp'd a deep, af-fect-ed curt-sey, And out your
Macht, — doch du ver-beug-test dich nur hoh-nisch und ich ward
a tempo
rit.
laugh - - - - ter rip-pled clear. To
nichts als aus-ge-lacht. Und
mf accel.
Meno mosso
rit.
make my heart's pain e-ven great-er, Up to the last your tem-per
um mich dann noch mehr zu qua-len ver-bliebst du trot-zig bis zum
p
(rit.)
a tempo
dolce
held, — And, as I would not beg for-give-ness Your kiss at
Schluss; Trotz al-lem Bit-ten, al-lem Fle-hen Ward zur Ver-
a tempo
dolce

rit. Tempo I *p*

part - ing you with - held. But pray don't think that when I

soh - nung mir kein Kuss. Nur, Teu - er - ste, darfst du nicht

rit.

f

left you I took my life in grim de - spair: Oh,

den - ken, dass ich mich drum er - schie - ssen würd'. du

rit.

no! I've pass'd thro' times like these Oft be - fore, my la - dy proud and

meinst, du seist mein er - stes Lieb - chen, doch nein, da hast du dich ge -

rit. *ff*

Allegro molto

fair! ——————

irrt! ——————

f giocoso *mf*

THE SIREN
(SIRENE)

Translated from the Russian of BALMONT by Frederick H. Martens
German version by S. König

(Original Key)

ALEXANDER GRETCHANINOFF
(1864-)

fond pas-sion braves, With such eyes the Si-ren the
Arg - - list be - wegt, mit Au - gen gleich die - sen be -
cresc.
heart. e'er en - chant - - - - - - - - - - eth.
strickt die Si - re - - - - - - - ne.
f
p
rit.
ff rit.
And
Und
pleggiere
soft and low sound - eth, and ten - der the voice That
mit ih - rer Stim - me, so sanft und so weich ver -

lur - eth the sea - man, o'er wild wa - ters
lockt sie den Schif - fer im Wel - len - ge -

cresc.

f

tak - en. 'Tis your ver - y own, and it
trie - be; wie ist die - se Stim - - me der

mf

p

seems to re - joice With mirth pure — and child - like, with
dei - nen doch gleich, bald un - schulds - voll kind - lich, bald

ff

love's long - ing shak - en! And
zit - ternd — vor Lie - be. Und

e'er when his bark strikes and staves on the
wenn dann sein Fahr - zeug am Fel - sen zer -
tempestoso
ff
rocks That ma - gic song, drown - ing, The
schellt, um - schmei - cheln den Sin - ken - den
sail - or en - chant - eth, And laugh - ter se -
lo - cken - de Tö - ne, ver - füh - re - risch'
p
duc - tive his a - go - ny mocks,
La - chen in's Ohr ihm dann gellt,

The laugh of the
und mit dei - nem
cresc. poco a poco
Si - ren your own laugh - ter haunt - eth, your
La - chen, und mit dei - nem La - chen lacht
own laugh - ter haunt
dann die Si - re
ff
sempre ff
Ossia:
eth.
ne.
ten a piacere
eth.
ne
più mosso
sf

FAR ON THE ROAD WE TWO JOURNEYED TOGETHER

(Original Key, E♭ minor)

Translated from the Russian
of D.U.TSERTELEV
by Constance Purdy

M.IPPOLITOFF-IVANOFF, Op.44, № 5

f
f
a tempo
num-bers came crowd-ing. But we dared not
mf cr - - - mf
mf an - - - do
f a tempo
voice them, dared not voice them, So si - len - ces
p
mf
p
fell. And now that I would, that I
mf
p
p

once more would say them: Our ways are di-vid-ed and bro - ken the spell.
How can I? How can I? But one word a-lone now is
left me, But one word is left me, and that is of

p
pp
all words the sad - dest,
of all words the sad - dest:
Fare-
mf
p
well!
Fare - well!
Fare - well!
pp
p

ONCE THERE LIVED A KING
(ALSATIAN BALLAD)

Translated from the Russian
by Constance Purdy

M. IPPOLITOFF-IVANOFF, Op. 15, No. 3

Allegretto grazioso

PIANO

mf

Meno mosso

mf

Once there lived a King, both old and poor was he, One daugh-ter left of all his treas-ures vast ac-crued— fair Ger - trude. Near them dwelt young Har - old, a

p

mf

p
no - ble knight and val - iant, Who scorn - ing oth - er maids and pleas - ures
mf
loved and wooed Sweet Ger - trude.
f
All their hopes proved
dross and, a - las! they loved in vain.
Fight - ing for the
Cross the knight by Sar - a - cens was slain — And she from that day forth —

p
doth yearn for his re - turn to Ger - trude.
f
Day and night thro' dark and light, and in and out of sea - son,
Ev-er doth she
wait, and grief has robb'd her of her rea - son And she from that day forth
doth yearn for his re - turn to Ger - trude
mf
p

Largo
p
Once there lived a King, both old and poor was he, One daugh-ter left of
mf
p
all his treas-ures vast ac - crued— fair Ger - trude So in my
p poco a
poco rall. e morendo
pp
ppp
coun-try runs the song.
Allegretto grazioso
fz
mf
p
pp

ROMANCE

Original Russian text translated from the Spanish by V. Botkine
English version by Constance Purdy

M. IPPOLITOFF-IVANOFF
Op. 23, Nº 3

And com-fort cool breez-es are bring-ing. Let now thy smile en-
chant-ing, My spir-it's fe-ver a-bat-ing, Shine down on me, Zo-
rai-ya, Come at my call, thy lov-er is
wait-ing. Come forth, my be-lov-ed, my fair Zo-
L. H.
R. H.

mf
f
rai - ya! Here I lan - guish fill'd with long - - - ing.
p
mf
p
To lands where the palm-trees are grow-ing. With thee would I fly far a -
way, Where on her own shore bloom-ing lone - ly The lo-tus-flow'r
gen-tly doth sway. In our tent we will rest, While the

sun's rays are burn - ing. Come then, come then, Zo - rai - ya,
L H
For thee, my love, thy lov - er is yearn - ing. Come
forth, my be - lov - ed, My fair Zo - rai - ya, Here I
lan - guish fill'd with long - - - ing!

YOU BROUGHT ME FLOWERS

Translated from the Russian
of LOUKIANOFF by Deems Taylor

(Original Key)

MYRON JACOBSON, Op 2, № 3

Moderato assai

VOICE

PIANO

sempre legato

p

rit.

p

a tempo

You brought me flow'rs, the fair - est and the last... I bent my head, and crush'd them with my kiss - es; Your kiss-es

espressivo

too, there on the pet - als lay. And now we two re-call the

past with long - - ing.

a tempo *mf* Oh, bit - ter hour! Star-ing a -

far you gaze, un-see-ing eyes with si-lent weep-ing blind - ed.. Ah,

f
God of mine! What dreams re - turn, what
phan - tom pas - sions rise From these pale, dy - ing
rit.
rit.
a tempo
ro - - - - - - ses!
a tempo
p
p
ppp

THE LABORER'S PLAINT
(MÉDITATION DU LABOUREUR)

Translated from the Russian
of KOLTSOFF by Grace Hall
French version by Mme. Alexandroff

A. KOPYLOFF

(Original Key)

friend ly hand Lifts my heav - y load. Nei - ther goods nor gold,
seul a - mi, Pour me se - cou - rir Point de piè - ces d'or
Nei - ther hearth nor cot, Faith - ful horse or dog
Gars sans feu ni lieu, Le che - val te man - que
Soothe my drear - y lot. One lone her - i - tage Did to
Et la herse aus - si J'ai re - çu pour - tant De mon
me be - long, One my fa - ther gave: Man - hood
père un bien, Mon tré - sor u - nique: U - ne

brave and strong. But this bit - ter toil, Hun-ger, need and cold, Far from
for - ce mâle. Mais le dur be - soin De ga - gner mon pain Hors de
p
home have made Me un - time - ly old.
mon vil - lage A mi - né la for - ce.
Des - o - late, a - lone, In the dark I sigh; By sad thoughts be - set, Un - to
Ah, com-ment, mon Dieu, Vivre ain - si tout seul? Ce à quoi je songe A ma
Heav'n I cry.
table as - sis.
pp

THE SMITH

(Original Key, D minor)

Translated from the Russian
by Constance Purdy

A. KORESTSCHENKO, Op. 42, No. 3

cresc.

sing - ers may I vie, Tho' I ri - val smiths de - fy; I was born a smith to be; strong and free!

cresc. *sf* *f* *dim.* *p* *poco*

With the forge a-blaze, my

breast
Holds no words
and knows
no
rest;
Largamente
To
my
song
my
ham
mer
swings,
f
7
For
a
way
it
sor
row
flings.
Sparks in
air
scat
ter
sf

care.
dim.
p mezza voce
Thee I fain would love full well, But in
cresc.
pp
brawn naught soft can dwell rough my ways
ff
mp
Grim is my ca - ress, and bleak, Words of
mf
cresc.

love I can - not speak, or ___ sweet phrase. Some - thing

says to my _ de - sire: Stern thy na - ture and se -

vere; ___ Ten - der words are not thy sphere. To thy fire! ___

Bet - ter far the ham - mer's sound. ___ With thy

cresc.
two hands strong and like Hearts of iron with steel bound
round, Strike! Strike!
ff
accelerando
quanto possibile
sf

STARS ETHEREAL
(KLARE STERNELEIN)

(Original Key)

Translated from the Russian
of K. FOFANOFF by Constance Purdy
German version by Lina Esbeer

BASIL KALINNIKOFF
(1866-1901)

Un poco più vivo
leaf - let with rap - ture thrill'd.
Laub - blatt, sich sehnt nach Ruh.
f
mf
p
rall.
p a tempo
p
And the dew - la - den
Und die Blu - men be -
blos - soms that ver - y night,
rau - schet vom Thau der Nacht,
Told the tales to the winds that were pass - ing by,
sie er - zäh - len dem Win - de die Mär - chen schnell,

And— the mu - ti - nous winds sang them joy - ous - ly O-ver land,
und— der Wind tragt sie fort, ei - ne leich - te Fracht ü-ber's Land,
o-ver sea, o-ver rock - y height.
ü-ber's Meer, ü - ber Fels - ge-röll.
ritardando
Meno mosso
And the earth 'neath the warmth of spring's ca - ress, In her fair wo - ven
Und die Er - de von Len - zes-lust hoch ge-schwellt pran-get fröh - lich in
Meno mosso
p

gar - ment of green-er - y, Pour'd the tales of the stars and their ten - der-ness
lich - tem Sma - rag - den-glanz, und er - füllt mir mit Mär - chen der Ster - nen-welt
O'er my soul in the thrill of love's ec - sta - sy.
die nach Lie - be sich seh - nen - de See - le ganz.
8
poco rit.
Tempo I
Con moto
In these days when my
Und zur trau - ri - gen
p

spir - it is sore op-press'd In the dark of these nights drear and sor - row-ful
herbst - li - chen Jah - res - zeit, bin in stür - mi - schen Näch - ten ich ganz al - lein,
espressivo
rit.
a tempo
I give back to you, stars clear and beau - ti - ful, All your tales with their
dann er - zähl' ich euch wie - der, ihr Ster - ne - lein, eu - re sin - ni - gen
molto rit
a tempo
won-der of depth and rest.
Mär-chen von Freud' und Leid.
rit
p

Original Russian text by A CHOMIAKOFF
English version, translated from the French
of M. D. Calvocoressi, by Constance Purdy

NOCTURNE

S. LIAPOUNOFF, Op 14, No3
(1859-)

mf

Calm and blest sea - son when love is ful - fill'd,

Earth, air and heav - en with ra - di - ance fill'd,

pp

Waves ev - er rest - - less their

pp mormorando

tu - - mult have still'd,
mf
And o - - - - - cean lies
dream - - - ing.
p

poco rit
Peace - ful my spir - it, land lies re-mote,
a tempo
As tho' en - chant - ed slum - bers my boat, Its
droop'd sails in - clin - - - ing.

mf
Skies like the o - cean their great vi - gil keep,
dolce
mf
Like un - to heav'n blue spar - kles the deep.
pp
Fath - - om - less heav'n and
pp

o - - - cean's wide sweep.
mf
A - like clear and
shin - - ing.
Poco più mosso
a piacere
O that my
colla parte

soul might find qui - et and rest!
O that less of - ten were earth - ly her quest On dreams
false de - pend - ing!
rit.
p

Tempo I
Rath - - - er than
dolciss.
mir - - - ror'd in az - ure blue sea
Would that, star - - glow - - - ing mys -
te - - - rious, in me
mf
mf

Heav'n e - ter - - - nal re -
flect - ed might be In beau - - -
ty un - - end - - - - ing!
f
f
accel.
dim.
rit.
p

CHRISTMAS SONG

Translated from the Russian
of A. KORINFSKY by Constance Purdy

S. LIAPOUNOFF, Op. 51, Nº 1

scat - ter'd un-der grow-ing pines, Word doth fol-low word, and bright
poco rit.
Poco più animato
p
weave the song in flow-ing lines. Like a check-er'd ta - ble-cloth
poco rit.
p
spread - ing out al - lur - ing - ly,
mf
Spar-kling gold and sil - ver both
mf
f
thread-ing it en - dur - ing-ly.
f
8

Tempo I
p
Soft the lit - tle car - ol blest sings the praise of home - land fair,
p
Spins from snow-drops, rasp - ber - ries, cur-rants kiss'd by sun and air,
8
f
Far from gar - dens flow'r-ing green swift to o-cean deep it flies,
f
From blue sea to sea to where flash - ing tur-rets steep a - rise;

p dolce

To her case-ment soar - ing free· thro' all bars that strong im - pede,

p dolce

cresc.

Nor of stair or path to guide doth the wing - ed song have need!

cresc. *f*

Poco meno mosso

p

Whis-pers to her heart laid bare,

floods its depths with shin - ing light.

Poco più mosso
pp scherzando
Guess, oh, guess what maid-en fair, round thy heart is twin - ing bright!
pp scherzando
sf
Tempo I
mf
And from heart of lov - ing maid to the youth's so
p
mf
f poco allarg.
fine and bold, Sweet the joy-ful car - ol sings, pure as sil-ver's chime on
poco allarg.
f
a tempo
gold.
dolce
8
pp

DEAR LOVE
(LIEB LIEBCHEN)

(Original Key, B♭ minor)

Russian original from a German text
Translated from the German
by Constance Purdy

NICOLAI MEDTNER, Op. 12, No. 1
(1879-)

f
hid - den shrine! There - in dwells a car-pen - ter grim and spare,
Kam - mer - lein? Du hau-set ein Zim-mer-mann schlimm und arg,
mf
poco calando
He's ham-m'ring for me a
Der zim-mert mir ei-nen
cantabile
poco calando
cof - fin there.
To - dten - sarg.
a tempo
mf
He
Es
a tempo
mf
meno f
knocks and he ham-mers by day and by night: Long since has he
häm - mert und klop-fet bei Tag und bei Nacht, Es hat mich schon
meno f

f

put sleep and rest to flight, — O car-pen-ter, thy work

längst um den Schlaf ge-bracht. — Ach, spu-tet euch, Mei-ster

f

p *cresc.*

fin-ish fast, — That soon — I may —

Zim-mer-mann, — Da-mit — ich bal-

p *cresc.*

f

— find sleep — at

de schla- fen

accel.

last! —

kann! —

con strepito

I HAVE COME TO SAY GOOD MORNING

(Original Key, F♯)

Translated from the Russian of A. FET by George Harris Jr

NICOLAI MEDTNER, Op. 24, No 8 (1879-)

Gai - ly wak - ing— here a feath - er, There a leaf the breeze is shak - ing,
più dolce
All a-thirst for spring-time weath - er;
poco calando
p poco meno mosso
And to tell thee how my pas - sion, As last night a -
cresc.
fresh I met thee, Ev - er strives for some new fash - ion
mf

dim e poco riten
Where - by I can well pro - tect thee;
poco riten
dim.
poco a poco a tempo
p
And to tell how
sempre animato
spring be - sets me, With so sweet a se - cret burn - ing That no words of
sempre animato
f
mine it lets me Sing,
f
p subito

cresc. ed affrettando
ex - cept with
its own yearn - - ing.
f
riten.
riten. poco
a tempo
f perdendosi
p
f cantabile
accel.
leggierissimo
dim.
p

MAY SONG
(MAILIED)

JOHANN WOLFGANG von GOETHE
Translated by Constance Purdy

NICOLAI MEDTNER, Op. 6, No 2
(1879-)

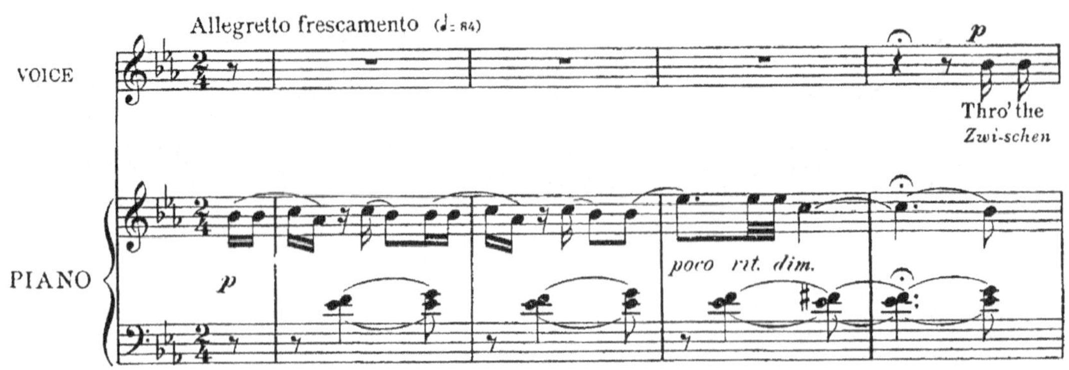

crescendo con violenza
mf
mil-let and corn, By the hedge-row and thorn, 'Twixt the trees and the hay,
Wai-zen und Korn, zwi-schen Hec-ken und Dorn, zwi-chen Baü-men und Gras
crescendo con violenza
mf
pleno f
poco ritenuto dimin.
O where goes she, tell me, pray?
wo geht's Lieb-chen, sag mir das!
a tempo
pleno f
poco ritenuto dimin.
mf
p
poco cresc. ed agitato
f
dim.

For my sweet - heart was not home, Gold-en Locks the
Fand mein Hold - chen nicht da-heim, muss das Gold - chen
a tempo
poco rit.
p
crescendo
ritenuto dim.
fields must roam, Green and ra-diant, flow-ring May Draws my dar-ling free and
drau-ssen sein; grünt und blu-het schön der Mai, Lieb-chen zie-het froh und
crescendo
ff
mf
gay.
frei
Tempo I
ten.
ten.
p
OSSIA

p
crescendo
On the rocks by the stream, Where that
An dem Fel - sen beim Flus, wo sie
ten.
ten.
crescendo
con violenza
f
ff
poco rit.
first kiss su-preme She be - stow'd up - on me, I see some - thing.
reich - te den Kuss, je - nen ers - ten im Gras, sah ich et - was.
f
ff
poco rit.
Is it she?
Ist sie das?
a tempo diminuendo
p leggierissimo

To Fraulein Hedwig Friedrich

SOLITUDE
(EINSAMKEIT)

(Original Key, D)

JOHANN WOLFGANG von GOETHE
Translated by Robert H Hamilton

NICOLAI MEDTNER, Op. 18, №3
(1879 -)

mp
cresc.
wis - dom, And the lov - er be pleased that
lehr - ung und dem Lie - ben - den gönnt dass
mp
OSSIA
f
dim
he en-com-pass his joy To you have the gods giv - en
ihm be - geg - ne sein Glück. Denn euch ga - ben die Göt - ter
cresc.
f
dim.
mp
what they de - nied un - to mor - tals: Grant that all in
was sie dem Men - schen ver - zag - ten: Jeg - li - chem, der
pp
you who trust rich in your com - fort may be
euch ver - traut hülf - reich und trost - lich zu sein.
pp

FIRST LOSS
(ERSTER VERLUST)

(Original Key, B minor)

JOHANN WOLFGANG von GOETHE
Translated by Constance Purdy

NICOLAI MEDTNER, Op. 6, No 8
(1879-)

ML - 2959 - 3

meno f
Who'll for me one brief hour bor - row From that hap - py
ach, wer bringt nur ei - ne Stun - de je - ner hol - den
meno f
dim.
time of yore!
Zeit zu - rück!
dim.
p
p poco
Lone - ly do I
Ein - sam nähr' ich
f
p poco
a poco cresc. ed agitato
nurse my sor - row, And with e'er re - new - ing an - guish
mei - ne Wun - de und mit stets er - neu - ter Kla - ge
a poco cresc. ed agitato

f sostenuto
Mourn for joy that is no more,
traur' ich um's ver - lor' - ne Glück.
f sostenuto
meno f
Ah, who will the days so love - ly Of that hap - py time re -
Ach! Wer bringt die schö - nen Ta - ge, je - ne hol - de Zeit zu -
poco riten.
meno f
poco riten.
store!
rück!
a tempo
p
f
p
pp

AH, NOT WITH GOD'S THUNDER

(Original Key)

Translated from the Russian of Count A.K TOLSTOY by Constance Purdy

MODEST MOUSSORGSKY (1839-1881)

cloud - lets from the heav-ens clear; Then did grim af - flic-tion sow the fin-est rain,
poco cresc.
pp
Sow the fin - est rain of Au - tumn dress, And it sow'd the rain
poco a poco accel.
mf
ver - y long a - go, And it beats and beats un-ceas - ing - ly,
poco a poco accel
sf
cresc.
Un - ceas-ing-ly, un - tir - ing - ly, end-less - ly it beats, nor stops to rest.
poco rit.

Tempo I
accel.
Al-though sat - ed, af - flic - tion fells the oak and strips it bare,
f
p
accel.
Plucks off all the leaves and twigs! Then straight to oth-ers where
f
p
accel.
mf
accelerando
cresc.
once dwelt hap-pi-ness, On-ward flies af - flic - tion in the tem - pest's blast,
accelerando
ff allargando e con forza
precipitando
And leav - ing the oak up - root - ed rolls a - way.
f allargando
sf
ff

To Anna Yakovlevna Vorobieff-Petroff

CRADLE SONG

Songs and Dances of Death, № 2

(Original Key)

Translated from the Russian
of Count A. Golenistcheff-Koutouzoff
by Constance Purdy

MODEST MOUSSORGSKY
(1839-1881)

Moderato tranquillo
a mezza voce
Ear - ly at break of day some one ap-proach-es, Death, the mer-ci-ful, knocks.
pp
f agitato
dim.
Hark! Trem-bling she turns, and at sight of him shud-ders.
agitato
sf cresc.
Lento funesto
Why dost thou fear me, my friend? See thro' the win-dow the pale morn is creep-ing.
p
f
accel.
Weep-ing and watch-ing and love thy soul have wear - ied, Come
sfp accel.

rest now a mo - ment, I will keep watch in thy stead, I will thy child soothe to
deep dream-less slum - ber, Sweet-er than thine is my song.
cantabile, rall
colla voce
Agitato patetico
pp
"Si-lence! my child hast thou wa-ken'd moan - ing! An - guish is rend - ing my
heart!" Soon in my arms he'll be peace-ful-ly sleep-ing: Hush-a-by, by-oh, by-low!
Lento funesto
allargando
p

Agitato
"Pal-er his cheeks grow and weak-er his breath-ing! Ah, now I pray thee, be
Lento
allargando
still!" These are good signs and his suf-f'ring will les-sen: Hush-a-by, by-oh, by-low.
allargando
Agitato
con dolore
dim.
"Forth, thou ac-curs-ed one! With thy ca-ress-es All of my joy thou hast robb'd!" Nay,
sf
sf
pp

Lento
tranquillo

allargando

peace - ful sleep to thy child I am bring - ing. Hush - a - by, by - oh, by - low!

p

allargando

Agitato con dolore

"Pit - y, have pit - y, O Death, cease but a mo - ment Sing - ing thy ter - ri - ble

cresc.

To César Cui

DARLING SAVISHNA
(SAVICHNA, MA LUMIÈRE)

(Original Key, C)

Translated from the Russian
of MODEST MOUSSORGSKY by Constance Purdy
French version by J. Sergennois

MODEST MOUSSORGSKY
(1839-1881)

fal-con bright and pure, Dar-ling Sa-vish-na, sweet I - van-ov-na,
mon fau - con ché - ri, Bel - le Sa-vich-na, mon I - va-nov-na,
From the beg-gar poor do not turn a-way, Drear-y lies my way,
Ne te las-se pas de ton va-nu-pieds, Prends pi - tié de mon
wretch-ed night and day! For the sport of men, look you born was I,
sort, de mes tour-ments! Je suis né, vois-tu, vil ho-chet des gens,
For their laugh-ter, ah, yes, to kiss their rod! They call, Sa - vish - na,
Pour le ri - re des au - tres, pour leurs jeux! On dit, Sa - vich - na,

me the fool for-lorn, Lis-ten, prais-ing me: "Va-nia, child of God!"
c'est un pau-vre fou, Et l'on m'a nom-me: Le cé-les-te Jean!
mf
f
mf
p
Dar-ling Sa-vish-na, sweet I-van-ov-na, Cuffs and kicks they give
Bel-le Sa-vich-na, chère I-va-nov-na, Le bous-cu-lent-ils,
sf
sf
mf
mf
p
Va-nia, child of God, With blows hon-or me, nour-ish me with scorn-
Le ce-les-te Jean, Le nour-ris-sent-ils de leur coups de pied!
p
p
p
But on hol-i-days, all in brave ar-ray, And with rib-bons deck'd,
Mais aux jours de fête où l'on sort pa-ré de ru-bans é-cla-
f
f
mf

ru - by red and gay, To poor Va - nia they give a bit of bread,
tants, de fleurs, d'oi - seaux, On lui donne un pain à ce pau - vre Jean,
So that on that day Va - nia shall be fed, Dar - ling Sa - vish - na,
A ce fou di - vin, le cé - les - te Jean. Bel - le Sa - vich - na,
O my fal - con bright, Give thy love to me, ug - ly tho' I be,
Ma lu - mière à moi, Ai - me moi, quoi - que laid, in - firme et nu,

Speak kind words to me, lost in mis - er - y! Nev - er love like mine
Don - ne - moi ton coeur, à moi qui vais seul! Moi qui t'ai - me comme
has on earth been known, Dar - ling Sa - vish - na, hear me, O my own,
on n'ai - ma ja - mais, O ma Sa - vich - na, qu'on me croie ou non,
Sweet I - van - ov - na!
Mon I - va - nov - na!
sf
mf
p
pp
ppp

To Vladimir Vassilevitch Nikolsky

GATHERING MUSHROOMS

(AUX CHAMPIGNONS)

CHANSONNETTE

(Original Key, D)

Translated from the Russian of L. MEY by Constance Purdy
French version by J. Sergennois

MODEST MOUSSORGSKY
(1839-1881)

sfz
cresc.
f
sfz
That for once at least a - ble. They may set a feast ta - ble.
Ser - rent moins la bour - se, les jours où l'on fait la fê - te.
mf
sfz
p
f
cresc.
p
But for thee, thou mean,— hat - ed,
Mais pour toi que j'ab - hor - re,
sfz
p
pp
mf
Wretch - ed do - tard, lean,— sat - ed, Toad-stools I'm ar - rang - ing, that
Vieux, ché - tif et ma - lin - gre, C'est par la fe - nê - tre que
sfz
pp
mf
sfz pp
Poi - son - ous, de - cay - ing, at Once for thy a - base - ment, I'll
tou - te la cor - beil - le de cham - pi - gnons pour - ris, ra - bou -
sfz
pp

thrust with - in the case - ment, While greed - y he to try of them
gris i - ra trou - ver ton gro - gnon; Poi - son des mou - ches, le
Quick - ly he shall die of them.
vieux é - tran - gle s'il y mord.
But for thee, my pale lov - er,
Et pour toi, mau - dit hom - me,
I will hill and dale cov - er Till I find a lawn, flow - er'd,
Tê - te blonde au front pâ - le, Je re - cherche une her - be soy -

Smooth and green, with - drawn, bow-er'd, Fra - grance for thy
eu - se,un fin ga - zon ten - dre, Cou - che molle et
pp
2 Ped.
sleep shed-ding Oak boughs o'er - head deep spread-ing, Night the
dou - ce que la nuit cou - vre d'om - bre sous des ri -
f
ppp
2 Ped.
match - ma - ker send - ing me. I a wid - ow tend - - - ing
deaux de feuil - la - ge frais, où som - meil - le la veu -
ff sfz
sfz
sf
f sfz
thee.
ve.
f
p

To Nikolas Rimsky-Korsakoff

HOPAK

Translated from the Russian of L. MEY by Constance Purdy
French version by Rodolphe Gaillard

MODEST MOUSSORGSKY
(1839-1881)

Now he's old and weak and ailing, Clumsy, red of pate and failing. That's my fate till now, alack! Hoi!
Il est vieux, il est bien usé, et vraiment j'en suis lassée, j'aime mieux d'autres compagnons! Hoi!
p
sf
cresc.
f
staccato
mf
Fortune frowns tho' long I've sought her! Here, old graybeard, fetch the water.
Des chagrins vient la révolte, Vieux, pour toi, l'eau est bien bonne,

p
I am for the tav - ern bound
Au ca - ba - - ret moi je m'en vais
sf
Just to catch the wel - come sound
Eh! la, a boi - re par i - ci
sf
Of the glass - es mer - ry clink, while
Ah! le joy - eux glou - glou, la bel -
sf
there I drink!
le chan - son
sf
sf
f
First one's hard and burns her lips!
Dès le pre - mier ver - re, joie!
f
sf
sf
f

Down the sec - ond soft - ly slips; Off she trips to
puis au se - cond, un, deux, trois, Gai - ment les pieds
sf
mf
p
mf
join the reels, With a young man at her heels. And old red pate,
s'a - gi - tent, la joy - eu - se s'é - lan - ce Que le vieux chez
f
how she mocks him, When he calls she on - ly mocks him:
lui l'ap - pel - le, en ri - ant el - le ré - pond:
"You old de-mon, now you re wed You must earn my dai - ly bread. That's what!
Pour ta fem-me tu m'as pri-se, com-me je suis, prends-moi donc! Hoi! hop!

f
And the chil-dren you must feed, Clothe and give them what they need. That's how!
Toi gar-de bien la mai-son, Moi je veux a-voir la paix Hoi! hop!
f
mf sf sf
If you dont, see here, you'll rue it, For I'll find a way to do it, Heed that!
Tra-vail-le bien pour les en-fants et de mê-me pour ta fem-me, Hoi! hop!
f
Now be quick, you shame-less sin-ner, Find the mon-ey for our din-ner,
Ne les lais-se man-quer de rien, si non, gare à toi, mon a-mi!
sf sf
f dolce
Here now! If you will re-pen-tance show Rock the cra-dle
Hoi! hop! Et, mon vieux, fais at-ten-tion, dou-ce-ment ber-
f p

to and fro, So now! Swing the cra - dle
ce l'en - fant, Hoi! hop! A - fin de ne

pp

slow - ly To and fro, So now!
pas ___ l'é - veil - ler Hoi! hop!

p *pp* *rit.*

Meno mosso

In the days when I was young-er, Yes, and right _ pleas-ing, too!
Lors-que j'é - tais en - cor li - bre, sans sou - ci du len - de - main,

mf

I would put a - way my a - pron When my dai - ly toil was thro'.
Ah! com-bien ri - ante et vi - ve, je cou - rais par les che - mins.

From my win-dow I'd nod smil-ing With my silks the time be-guil-ing-
A-vec cha-cun, Ah! oui, vrai-ment, je m'a-mu-sais, tou-jours gai-'ment.
Più mosso
f
Come, my friends, you Johns and Si-mons! Go and don your coats, my fine ones!
Eh! là, Si-mon, Eh! là, I-van! Vite, en-trons et que l'on dan-se,
f
mf
f
mf
poco a poco accel.
Off we'll set in fin-est feath-er, Walk and talk and sing to-geth-er!
Et joy-eux le temps pas-se-ra, al-lons, bu-vons, que l'on chan-te!
mf
Hoi! Hoi! Hoi! Hoi!
Hoi! Hop! Hoi! Hop!
f
f
mf

Tempo I

Hoi! Hoi! Hoi! Hoi! Hoi! Hoi! For the gay Ho-pak!
Hoi, hoi, hoi, hoi, hoi, hoi, hop, hop, hop, dan-sons!

mf *sf* *sf* *sf*

Once I loved a fine Cos-sack! Now he's old and
J'ai pour ma-ri un co-sa-que, Il est vieux, il

sf *sf* *sf* *sf* *sf*

weak and ail-ing, Clum-sy, red of pate and fail-ing,
est bien u-sé, Et vrai-ment j'en suis las-sé-e,

sf *sf* *sf* *sf* *sf*

That's my fate, too true, a-lack! Hoi!
j'aime mieux d'au-tres com-pa-gnons! Hoi!

sf *sf* *sf* *sf*

To Alexander Sergeievich Dargomyjsky

JEREMOUSCHKA'S CRADLE SONG

(Original Key, F♯)

Translated from the Russian of NEKRASSOFF by Constance Purdy

MODEST MOUSSORGSKY (1839-1881)

p
pp
dim.
Free from grief his life may spend.
Bye-low, bye, bye, Bye-low, bye, bye.
(Ba - yon, baï, baï, Ba - yon, baï, baï,)
pp
dim.
ppp
p
E - ven straws must break at might's com - mand,
p
So to might thy head bow low,
And with all the great-est in the land
dim.
Soon in fa - vor thou shalt grow.
Bye-low, bye, bye, Bye-low, bye, bye.
(Ba - yon, baï, baï, Ba - yon, baï, baï,)
pp
dim.
cresc.

cresc. *dim.* *p* *pp* *ppp*

Lords and la-dies all thy friends shall be, Wealth and fame their court shall pay.

While with youth and beau-ty joy - ous - ly, Thou shalt jest the live-long day.

Gai - ly then thy life,— free from care and strife, Hap-pi - ly—shall roll a-way.

Bye-low, bye,— bye, Bye - low, bye,— bye.
(Ba - yon, baï,— baï. Ba - yon, baï,— baï.)

CPSIA information can be obtained at www.ICGtesting.com
Printed in the USA
LVOW03*0752030315

429063LV00008B/21/P

9 781117 141282